INDIAN DIASPORA

Study of Emerging Sandwich Cultures

Foreword by
Prof. Yogesh Atal
Former Principal Director
Social and Human Sciences
UNESCO

Surendra K. Gupta

ATLANTIC
PUBLISHERS & DISTRIBUTORS (P) LTD

Published by
ATLANTIC
PUBLISHERS & DISTRIBUTORS (P) LTD
7/22, Ansari Road, Darya Ganj,
New Delhi-110002
Phones : +91-11-40775252, 23273880, 23275880, 23280451
Fax : +91-11-23285873
Web : www.atlanticbooks.com
E-mail : orders@atlanticbooks.com

Branch Office
5, Nallathambi Street, Wallajah Road,
Chennai-600002
Phones : +91-44-64611085, 32413319
E-mail : chennai@atlanticbooks.com

ISBN 978-81-269-1774-7

Printed in India at Nice Printing Press, A-33/3A, Site-IV, Industrial Area, Sahibabad, Ghaziabad, U.P.

Foreword

Social sciences in India began with researches on India, both by the expatriates and the native Indians. The outsiders studied them out of curiosity to know the strange land, its exotic customs, and the traditions and practices of the autochthones and of the complex Indian civilization that has assimilated traits and features from a wide variety of societal and cultural sources to evolve into a distinct entity. There was so much to be done here that even the native anthropologists forgot the very character of their discipline, namely study of "other" cultures.

The vast canvas of Indian society provided the researchers with functional equivalents of other cultures in its various regions and villages and tribal areas inhabiting remote and inaccessible lands. Such was the obsession with India, and that continues even today, that the same subject studied by an expatriate was called "anthropology", and the one studied by an Indian was termed "sociology". Such falsity made the distinction between the two disciplines somewhat superfluous.

On several occasions, I had hinted at the need for Indians to study society and cultures of other lands, but did not find many buyers. It then occurred to me that one such area to begin with can be the study of the Indians who have settled abroad. This was also studied by foreign scholars earlier. Adrian Mayer's name comes immediately to my reckoning who had not only studied a village in the Malwa region of India but also the Indians settled in Fiji. Then came the studies of Caste in overseas Indian communities[1]. Around that time also appeared a detailed study by Ravindra Jain of the Indians working on rubber plantations in Malaysia.

Reviewing Jain's *Eastern Anthropologist*, I was amazed at the richness of data lending itself to a theory and wondered as to why Jain limited himself to detailed descriptions as a good ethnographer. There occurred for the first time in me the idea of "sandwich cultures". I found that the Indians in Malaysia working on the rubber plantations were living simultaneously in two cultures—their parent culture in South India on the one side, and the host culture of Malaysia, on the other. In fact, there is a clear evidence in that book as to how these settlers in a strange land have been squeezed, nay sandwiched, between the twin pressures of the parent culture and the host culture. The wealth of information contained in that meticulously written book instigated me to coin the phrase "sandwich cultures".

With my assignment at UNESCO as its Principal Director of the Regional Unit for Social and Human Sciences in Asia and the Pacific, I got the golden opportunity to visit several countries not only of the Asia-Pacific region, but also of other parts of the world. Everywhere I found the ubiquitous presence of the itinerant Indian, and everywhere I noticed how diligently, knowingly or unknowingly, the carriers of Indian culture have made equations with the host cultures. Everywhere I discovered the "little India", but no two such configurations were identical.

While my UNESCO assignment did not permit me the luxury of carrying out intensive research on this hitherto undiscovered phenomenon, it did allow me to gather deep impressions of the emerging social reality for building up a conceptual apparatus. By this time, way back in the 1980s, Ravindra Jain's lead encouraged several others to study Indians living abroad, and following the academic fashion of the time, this new area came to be termed Indian diaspora studies.

1. Barton M. Schwartz, (ed.) *Caste in Overseas Indian Communities*: San Francisco, Chandler Publishing Co. 1967.

The editor of the *Sociological Bulletin* of the Indian Sociological Society approached me to do a paper on Indian diaspora for its special issue. I used that opportunity to prepare a conceptual paper on the sandwich cultures, and encouraged Professor Surendra K. Gupta—author of the present work, and his M. Phil student—my own daughter, Ruchira to conduct field research on this phenomenon in Thailand where I was based. Luckily, Gupta was awarded the ICSSR Senior Fellowship with provision to do fieldwork in Bangkok, and thus we worked together. He was inspired by my theoretical construct, and I was helped by his field data, as well as that of Ruchira, to chisel my conceptual artifact.

Now, nearly thirty years later, Surendra Gupta is bringing out this volume. This shows his continuing commitment to this area of research. It is also a testimony to the utility of my conceptual framework.

I only feel sad that despite my original article published in the *Sociological Bulletin* no other Indian scholar bothered to touch it while it got reprinted in an Australian journal, and the American Political Science Association devoted a special session in one of its annual conferences, sometime in the 1980s, to discuss my paper, even though I was not present there. Indians study Indians, but do not generally bother to acknowledge contributions of their compatriots. Their neglect has deprived me of learning about the weaknesses of the proposed paradigm. But then, that is my loss. However, I feel gratified that the concept is in vogue and some of the universities in India have included it in their syllabi.

Surendra Gupta is different; maybe, because he was my student. I hope that in time to come, the key points drawn by Gupta will be duly assimilated into my scheme to make it more specific in terms of certain generalizations. For example, the concept of duality-living in two cultures simultaneously is unique to the theory of sandwich cultures. People of such a culture are, by definition, bilingual, if not multilingual. But the linguistic competence in the two languages might vary. In Fiji I discovered that someone had published a book of grammar for Fiji Hindi. The newspapers and weeklies published in Hindi, that is devnagari script have a language that reads like the language of *Akash Vaani* (All India Radio) of the 1970s.[2] Names of the members of the sandwich cultures have a queer mix: those who have converted to Christianity, for example, have Christian names, but those who have not changed their religion use traditional names but their English spellings are different (see the full form of V.S. Naipaul or the former Prime Minister of Mauritius to note the difference). Colloquial language of the area from which the original migrants hailed is used with all its rusticity. These people use the language of their native place for conversation and communication, but may not be at ease writing it.

Similar ambivalence is found with regard to food. Outside the home, people prefer eating food that is generally not eaten at home. Even those persons, who claim to be vegetarians at home, become non-vegetarians outside. The increasing popularity of Indian restaurants is certainly not an evidence of growing demand amongst the Indian clientele—those settled there or those visiting from India. The eating joints attract non-Indian populations more often. The demand for Halal food, for example, has made Indian restaurants popular amongst the Middle Eastern Muslims, also because of food semblance. At home, the people living a sandwich culture somehow may combine the local with their parochial dishes. Where Indian populations are substantial, separate marketplaces are being operated to meet their specific needs as to victuals, clothing, jewelry, and items of worship.

Religion is one aspect that generally does not change. One can see the architectural marvels of temples, gurdwaras and mosques in many of these countries where huge crowds assemble on a regular basis. In fact, these places of worship can be

2. Now the language in the Indian media has become more Hinglish.

regarded as tutorial schools and agents of socialization for the uprooted populace that get re-linked to the place of their origin.

This function is now performed by the mass media as well. Through information and communication highways, programmes on Indian culture and religion are beamed to remotely located sandwich cultures of Indians. They introduce their audience both to India's past and the present. Without moving geographically they attain psychological mobility and develop a sense of empathy. Geography is no longer a stumbling block; roads of communication transport the diaspora to their cultural past and to their contemporary counterparts living in the parent culture. Of course, there are now increasing connections with the native land. But the globalization process has not only brought the world cultures to India, the country has also emerged in miniature in various countries of the globe and these twin processes have made sandwich cultures a viable proposition.

Marriage is yet another area where insulator mechanisms are at work. Sandwich culture people prefer generally to marry from among their co-habitants, or look for spouses from their caste of origin back in their parental home. Cross-cultural marriages do take place, but they are few and far between. Many priests have found this an outlet to go and settle in those countries to officiate at such ceremonies. They have been secondary carriers of Indian tradition to distant lands.

This book is not yet another empirical study of sandwich cultures. It is an attempt to feed my proposed scheme utilizing the researches done and reported in regard to Indians settled in Thailand, the United States of America, and the Caribbean Islands of Trinidad and Tobago. The various studies relative to these countries and carried out by scholars, both Indian and foreign, are couched in different theoretical frameworks or disciplinary orientations. Surendra Gupta had to wade through them to cull out points of relevance to the theory of sandwich cultures. It was a difficult task, particularly for a person of Surendra's calibre whose strength lies in solid and deep field research, and not on conceptualization. But I am glad that the outcome of his exercise is more than satisfactory. It should definitely provide leads to future researchers and encourage them to employ the sandwich cultures model while studying the diaspora, not only the Indians, but also of other cultural origins.

Professor Yogesh Atal
Former Principal Director
Social and Human Sciences,
UNESCO

Preface

Sometime in the mid-1980s I paid a visit to Bangkok based UNESCO Regional Unit for Social and Human Sciences for Asia and the Pacific, for short, RUSHSAP. I was on an assignment with RUSHSAP and spent nearly a month there. In Bangkok, I had the pleasure of staying with Professor Yogesh Atal, my teacher, who was the Director of the Regional Unit. Professor Atal was then writing a conceptual essay on the phenomenon of sandwich cultures on invitation from the *Sociological Bulletin*. We discussed the concept in fair detail, spending many evenings together.

Thailand is a place which is ideal for the study of multiple cultures living together, and offered a good opportunity to empirically test the formulation of sandwich cultures as propounded by Professor Atal. He encouraged me to plan a study. Happily, the proposal was approved by the Indian Council of Social Science Research for a Senior (post-doctoral) Fellowship. I returned to Thailand and spent more than two months to do the fieldwork. The book based on that research was published as *Indians in Thailand* (1999).

This book is a follow-up to that study coming after nearly 30 years. Meanwhile my interest in the subject has grown and I have read much material on what is called studies on Indian diaspora. Indians are scattered in most of the countries of the world, and now interest in studying them is growing among the Indian scholars as well.

It is sad, however, that while so many studies now exist, none of them has bothered to employ the seminal sandwich cultures paradigm proposed by Professor Atal. This has, in fact prompted me to scan them once again with a view to finding out whether they can be recast in terms of sandwich cultures theory. To attempt to review all the studies published so far and on various communities of Indian diaspora settled in different lands would have been a herculean task. That exercise would have been huge and perhaps beyond my capabilities to handle it singly.

I decided, therefore, to select one country each from the two Americas—Trinidad and the United States of America and compare the profiles of Indians settled there with that of the Thailand to answer the key question: How do Indian migrants develop an equation with the host societies?

These three countries represent three different continents, namely South America, Asia, and North America. The Indians in these countries also provide a varied picture, ranging from indentured labour settled in Trinidad, to the highly educated professionals in the United States of America. The Indians in Bangkok fall in between these two categories. Since the cultural, contextual, and situational conditions of all three streams of Indian diaspora in these countries are different, so are their sandwich cultures.

The study is the outcome of the Senior Fellowship awarded to the author for two years by the Indian Council of Social Science Research, New Delhi. During the course of Fellowship I was affiliated to the Nehru Memorial Museum and Library, New Delhi. My sincere thanks go to the Director and the staff of the library, especially to Shri Navin Mahajan, Assistant Librarian, for all the help and cooperation.

I have no words to express my gratitude to Professor Yogesh Atal who not only introduced me to the concept of sandwich cultures but also encouraged me to undertake this study.

I am grateful to Professor Atal for sparing his time from his busy schedule to go through the several drafts of the chapters and for giving useful suggestions. I am indebted to him for writing the Foreword to the book. I must also express my gratitude to Mrs Seema Atal for her generous hospitality and constant encouragement to complete the work.

My sincere thanks are also due to my secretaries Mrs Santhamma Mathew and Mrs Omana David, who helped prepare the manuscript for printing.

I owe a special debt to my wife, Dr Indira Gupta and our daughter Nayantara for all the support and encouragement.

My publisher, Mr Harjeet Singh of Atlantic Publishers and Distributors (P) Ltd., New Delhi, deserves thanks for agreeing to publish this work, and in record time.

Surendra K. Gupta

IASSI Headquarters
IIPA Hostel Building
Indraprastha Estate
New Delhi, 110002

Contents

Foreword ... *iii*

Preface ... *ix*

1. The Phenomenon of Sandwich Culture: Theoretical Framework ... 1-26

2. Trinidadian Indians ... 27-54

3. Hindus and Sikhs in the United States of America ... 55-90

4. Punjabis and Gorakhpuris in Thailand ... 91-128

5. Emerging Sandwich Cultures: A Comparative Perspective ... 129-148

Appendix: Trends of Indian Diasporic Studies 149-158

Endnotes ... 159-160

References ... 161-170

CHAPTER-1

The Phenomenon of Sandwich Culture: Theoretical Framework

Human migration is an age old phenomenon. All societies register demographic changes through the immigration of people from other societies and emigration of its members to other societies. These movements may be temporal or permanent; may be in small numbers or in large numbers. Arrival and departure of populations in a given society change its social and demographic structure and significantly affect its culture.

The processes of migration break "insulation" of societies. The immigrants get exposed to the host culture and the natives get exposed to some significant aspects of the parent culture of the migrant group—the language, dressing pattern, food habits and other observable practices. In the process, a series of transformations occur in the receiving society. Similarly, emigrants from the society carry with them certain cultural bag and utilise it in the process of their settling down in an alien culture; not only do they influence the host society but also get influenced by it and evolve a conciliatory cultural framework from the borrowing of alien traits and accommodating them in their parental culture. This phenomenon is named by Yogesh Atal as Sandwich Culture. He proposed this concept in his seminal paper titled *Outsiders as Insiders: The Phenomenon of Sandwich Culture*[1] (1989).

Atal argued that whatever may be the purpose and motivation of migration, the migrant group has to adapt to at least some cultural norms and practices of the host society. The arriving group makes judicious selection of traits from the cultural repertoire of the host society as part of the process of adaptation. Generally, people tend to accept those outside traits that are closer to their parent culture. Additionally, they are left with no option but to adopt those of the culture traits of the host culture that constitute its core and are indispensable for a better accommodative living in a strange milieu. The assimilation or integration of the emigrant group into the host society depends on the extent to which its members are able to adjust in the new cultural milieu, on the one hand, and the contact they are able to maintain with their parent society, on the other.

Assimilation of immigrants in the host society means near-complete loss of their own identity; it happens when the identity of outsiders and insiders is blurred. When a society does not accept migrants and maintains distance from them, the migrants have poor chances of assimilation. This situation continues despite the willingness on the part of migrants to become insiders. The situation is different when members from both the groups are ready to accept each other.

Theoretically, nine possibilities exist:

1. When migrants are willing to assimilate in the host society and the members of the host society are also willing to accept them as part of their core group.
2. When migrants are willing but only some members of the host society are willing.
3. When migrants are ready to assimilate and willing to be the part of the host society but host society is not willing to accept them.
4. When only some migrants are willing to assimilate and the host society is also ready to accept.
5. When only some migrants are willing to assimilate and only a small section in the host society is willing to accept them.
6. When only some migrants are willing to assimilate and none in the host society accepts them.
7. When migrants are not willing to assimilate but host society is ready to accept them.
8. When migrants are not willing but some people in host society are ready to accept them.

9. When migrants are not willing and host society is also not willing to accept.

This is shown in the following chart:

Chart # 1

Willingness of Migrants and Natives
Willingness of the Natives

Migrants Willingness	Willing to accept Y	Some willing S	Not willing N
Willing to assimilate Y	YY	YS	YN
Some willing S	SY	SS	SN
Not willing N	NY	NS	NN

Y-willing to assimilate, N-not willing to assimilate, S-some willing to assimilate.

In the first condition (YY) migrants assimilate in the host society forgoing their original identity; this happened, for example, when Europeans migrated to the United States of America. The host society became a "melting pot" and a new American culture took birth. Another extreme (cell 9 NN) case relates to a situation when both—natives as well as migrants—are unwilling to even intermingle as happened when indentured labour from India initially settled in Trinidad. Such societies have been identified as plural societies (Furnival, 1948). In such societies immigrants live side by side with the natives without mingling with them. People in such societies hold on to their distinctive culture, language, and beliefs and also pursue different economic activities. C.P. Siu called migrants who had no desire to participate in the community life of the host society, *Sojourners* (C.P. Siu, 1952). Chinese in the early phase of the United States of America belonged to this category.

The concepts of Sojourner and Plural Society are applicable to those migrant groups who maintain their separate cultural identity and who do not wish to integrate and assimilate into the host society. The word Sojourner itself suggests the temporal character of the migrant. About the concept of Plural Society, it is the contention of Atal (who told the author in a personal communication) that it was introduced to support the ideology of colonialism. Colonial powers were interested in keeping the various ethnic communities at a distance from each other to create divisions and thus to strengthen their hold over them.

They, therefore, laid emphasis on their "separateness" rather than on their "unison". It was used not only for the migrants, but also for regional regimes in India which were brought under a common colonial empire while maintaining their limited sovereignty, suggests Atal.

Migrants in the remaining cells of Chart 1, to adopt some aspects of the culture of the host society in order to settle permanently without assimilating and integrating into the host society. In such conditions, migrants become part of two cultures—their own parent culture, and the culture of the host society. Acculturation, in fact, has been accepted as the first step of integration and assimilation (see for example, S.N. Eisenstadt, 1954 and M.M. Gordon, 1964). While studying the absorption of immigrants in Israel, Eisenstadt found learning of various roles, norms and customs of the host society as essential part of accommodation. According to him, learning and "internalization" of various roles and habits includes language, dress, religious beliefs, economic practices and day-to-day behaviour.

While studying the assimilation of Negroes, Jews, Catholics (excluding Negroes and Spanish speaking Catholics) and Pureto Ricans, Gordon (1964) came to the conclusion that "(1) cultural assimilation or acculturation is likely to be the first of the types of assimilation to occur when a minority group arrives on the scene; and (2) cultural assimilation or acculturation of the minority group may take place even when the other type of assimilation occurs simultaneously or later and this condition of acculturation only may continue indefinitely" (1964: 77).

While studying the assimilation of Chinese in Thailand Coughlin (1960) coined the concept of *Double Identity*. When immigrants learn the language and some other cultural traits of the host society as a part of their acculturation process, they tend to develop a double identity: the Chinese residing in Thailand are both Thai and the Chinese. Their culture is a judicious mix of parent society and that of host society. They would describe their nationality as Thai, and their ethnic affinity as Chinese. Since assimilation and integration of any group in another group is a long drawn process, majority of the migrants remain sandwiched between the culture of the host society and that of the parent society. The culture emerging out of such an interaction has been named as *Sandwich Culture* (Yogesh Atal, 1989); the practitioners of a sandwich culture are characterised by double identity. Children of Indian parentage born in the US are jokingly, and at times pejoratively called ABCD, indicating American Born Confused Desi.

This book is an attempt to further explicate the phenomenon of Sandwich Culture with a view to enriching the concept as propounded by Atal. I found it useful in cross-cultural comparison. Based on already published material on the Indian Diaspora in some select countries, this study attempts to recast the data in the categories envisaged in the concept of Sandwich Culture.

As mentioned earlier, the concept of Sandwich Culture was proposed by Atal in an article titled: "Outsiders as Insiders: The Phenomenon of Sandwich Culture", published in *Sociological Bulletin* (Vol. 38, No. 1, 1989). It was discussed in a special session of one of the Annual meetings of the American Political Science Association in the 1990s. He first used this concept while reviewing Ravindra K. Jain's book *South Indians on the Plantations Frontier in Malaya* (1973). Earlier, in his Mahatma Gandhi Memorial Lecture delivered at the School of Oriental and African Studies, University of London in 1972, he employed the dual concepts of "Insulators" and "Apertures" to analyse the dynamics of nation building. These concepts became crucial elements for investigating the integrative mechanisms operating at any level—the nation or the subgroup/subculture within a community.

Migration of people, says Atal, exposes the host society to new "...men, material, and messages which are screened by a society's gatekeepers which permit or deny their entry. A society with powerful insulatory mechanisms may thwart all entries and maintain its pristinity; a complete breakdown of the insulators would result in the society's absorption into another bigger powerful system. This dynamics of interplay of a society's insulators and apertures determines its degree of integration" (Atal, 1989: 30). The term *Sandwich*, "refers to the process (as well as the product) of laying or placing something between two layers" (*ibid.*: 31). While referring to the culture of the migrant groups, he further writes: "A migrant to a society with a longer period of stay fits the description of a sandwich man carrying the two tags, one representing the country of the origin and the other the country of his migration" (*ibid.*: 31). He has cited many examples of migrants in different countries which fit his concept of sandwich culture. He also points out that "a sandwich culture…is...a subculture of the outside group settled in a different country/setting and thus contributing to the heterogeneity" (*ibid.*: 36).

Insulators and Apertures model, in fact, operates equally for migrants as well for the members of the host society. If a migrant group refrains from intermingling with the members of the host society, and if the members of the host society also have a similar attitude towards the outsiders, then both the groups create more insulators rather than open out apertures.

The concepts of plural societies and sojourners do not aptly accommodate the phenomenon of Sandwich Culture which talks of "…communities [that] have assumed double identities through shedding of some elements of their parent culture and adoption of host cultural elements with a view to assimilation. This dual process of pulls from two opposite directions, of orientation toward two cultures leads to accretions and attritions and develop a new pattern of interrelationship between different elements. Such an intercalation gives rise to *Sandwich Culture*" (*ibid.*: 33). Atal further writes that the concept of Sandwich Culture is applicable at various levels:

1. At the country level;
2. Within the country level:
   (a) Immigrant communities,
   (b) Autochthonous communities;
3. Frontier groups;
4. Refugee communities; and
5. Sandwich groups created as a result of relay migration (*ibid.*: 36).

One of the necessary conditions of sandwich culture is that the migrant group besides retaining some aspects of parent culture should also adopt some aspects of the culture of the host society. For sandwiching it is essential to be a part of both the cultures. Insulation from the host society will alienate and marginalize the group and may even face hostility as happened to Tamil migrants in Sri Lanka. Opening of apertures towards the host society and insulating from the parent culture would lead to assimilation and integration of migrants as happened to Indians who migrated to the regions of Southeast Asia in the thirteenth century. When both the groups insulate from each other, it will give birth to plural societies. In a tabular form it can be shown as below:

Host Society

Parent society	Insulators (I)	Apertures (A)
Insulators (I)	Conditions of plural society (I I)	Chances of assimilation (I A)
Apertures (A)	Migrants as marginalized group (A I)	Conditions of sandwich culture (AA)

In order to test and empirically verify the concept of sandwich culture two sets of factors which operate to facilitate or hinder the process of formation of sandwich cultures are insulatory mechanisms and aperture opening. The factors listed by Atal are as follows:

1. Aperture openings

Some of the possible apertures are:

(i) Intermarriage
(ii) Adoption of the language of the host culture
(iii) Religious conversion
(iv) Promotion of inter-commensality
(v) Adoption of food habits, and developing a taste for the host cuisine
(vi) Adoption of names of the host society.

2. Insulatory mechanism

The possible insulatory mechanisms listed by Atal are:

(i) Retention of mother tongue
(ii) Concentration of living quarters to promote greater interaction with the members of the group
(iii) Provision of separate educational facilities for the children
(iv) Practice of endogamy

(v) Concentration in certain occupations

(vi) Formation of voluntary organizations

(vii) Pursuit of parental religion

(viii) Continuation of food habits and taboos associated with eating

(ix) Retention of cultural diacriticals, particularly in the manner of dressing

(x) Racial features

(xi) Keeping apertures open to the parent culture in the form of:

(a) Frequent visits

(b) Schooling of children either in parent society or using the textbooks and reading material in separate schools

(c) Affinal relations

(d) Exposure to media, books, music, films

(e) Postal and telecommunication.

An attempt has been made in this study to work out the operation of these two sets of factors among the immigrants from India settled in various countries. The data on these sets have been culled out from the empirical studies available. But before discussing the methodology, objectives, and the hypotheses tested in this study, let us elaborate functioning of these factors.

II

Aperture Openings

Opening of apertures to the host society and at the same time to retain contact with the parent society is the necessary condition for sandwich culture. However, no group can afford to insulate completely; similarly, it cannot be fully exposed to the outside world. There are always degrees of exposure and/or insulation. Assimilation and absorption of an immigrant group in the host society may be the last resort, but before that all immigrants adopt some aspects of cultural traits of the host society during their sojourn. In other words, it can be said that all immigrants are sandwiched between the twin cultures of the host society and that of the parent society. It is also not easy for any immigrant group to completely disown their parent culture.

However, the degree and extent to which immigrants are sandwiched depends on the personality characters of the members of the immigrant group. Some members may be more inclined towards host society while others may resist the move. For instance, younger generation might be willing to adopt more aspects of host culture as compared to older generation. The size of the migrating group also affects this process; larger the size, slower the process of assimilation, and *vice versa.*

Assimilation of immigrants in host society will also depend on the attitude of the members of the host society. If the members of the host society are not favourably inclined to make the immigrants a part of in-group, immigrants will be sandwiched between the two cultures and the process of assimilation would be longer and painful. Some of them may make attempts to create more apertures to facilitate their early absorption. Sandwich culture of such group will be different from that of those who prefer to remain as sojourners.

Now, we shall discuss how the apertures listed by Atal in his model may affect the sandwich culture of migrants.

1. **Intermarriages:** Intermarriages between immigrants and the members of the host society would certainly open the way for assimilation of immigrants. But there are many bottlenecks in the process. Though their place of origin might be the same, the socio-economic and cultural, religious background of the immigrants may vary and their attitude towards host society may also differ. In such situations we may not find much intermarriage between the migrants and the host society. Sometime, intermarriages may be one-way process. For instance, immigrants may accept the girls of the host society as their daughters-in-law, but may not like to marry their daughters to the boys of the host society. There could also be a reverse process where immigrant girls are accepted as brides but daughters are not given to the "outsiders". In such cases, the immigrants will not be able to assimilate in the host society and will remain sandwiched between the host culture and the parent culture.

2. **Adoption of Names of the Host Society:** Adoption of names of the host society takes place under special circumstances. On occasions, immigrants change their names when they find that the members of the host society are unable to pronounce their names. In such cases, they shorten their names such as Bhupinder may become Bob. In some societies, it is mandatory for immigrants who have opted for the citizenship of the host society, to adopt a new name (for example, in Thailand). Adoption of names of the host society in most of the cases may be a formality and such names may generally be used only for official records and purposes. But in reality original name may be more frequently used in day-to-day communication.
3. **Adoption of Language of the host society:** Adoption of the language of the host society is a necessity for immigrants aspiring to settle down for a long period. The immigrants have to learn at least spoken language of the host society for day-to-day communication. The people of Indian subcontinent who migrated after India became independent did not face any such problem in English speaking countries such as USA, UK, Canada, or Australia and New Zealand, because English is taught as a second language in India. But when they migrate to other non-English speaking countries, they have to learn the language of the host country in order to communicate with the locals; those who go only as sojourners, however, can manage with English as most countries use this international language for communicating with the aliens. The point made here is that those aspiring to settle down in a different country than their own need to develop communication skills in a native language. Even the colonial masters who propagated their own language in the colonies governed by them felt the need for learning the local language to improve their governability. It will not be amiss to mention that in Australia and New Zealand, which are rightly described as countries of the migrants and where English—the native language of the

migrants who overwhelmed the local populace—is spoken by all irrespective of race or tribal affiliation, the aboriginal movement has pressurised the majority community to learn the native languages. In all official functions in New Zealand, for example, the New Zealanders open their remarks with a few sentences in Maori.

4. **Religious Conversion:** A migrant group may rarely opt for change in religion but where it occurs it becomes a clear indicator of integrative process—that of opening the religious aperture. When a religion does not permit conversion, it serves as an insulator—such may be the case with either religion, namely the religion of the immigrant community or the religion of the host society. Even when the religion permits conversion, the person or the group concerned might not opt for it. In such situations, the group maintains its separate identity. All rituals and religious ceremonies observed by the group clearly demonstrate their independence and separateness. It must, however, be said that the possibility of entry of certain elements from other religions into one's own religious world cannot be ruled out. One also notices the fact that people not belonging to a religion do partake in certain religious festivals of the non-membership group. Christmas and New Year are celebrated by non-Christians, for example. Similarly, Holi and Diwali festivals of the Hindus are also observed by the non-Hindus. Hindus greet Muslims on the Id festival. The Thais celebrate the New Year according to Gregorian calendar but follow the Buddhist year sequence. All these are instances of sandwiching.
5. **Promotion of Inter-Commensality:** Opening of apertures through inter-commensality between the migrants and the host society would indicate the acceptability of migrants by the host society and *vice versa*. Further strengthening of inter-commensality between both the groups may lead to integration. But if either of the group is not willing to develop inter-commensality relations, then the two groups will continue to maintain their

separate identity. Moreover, inter-commensality, like intermarriages may vary depending upon the socio-economic, cultural and religious background of the immigrants. Generation-wise variations, however, may also be observed. First generation immigrants may insulate themselves from the host society but the people of second and subsequent generations may open apertures through inter-commensality, leading to their integration into the host society.

6. **Adoption of Food Habits and Developing Taste for the Cuisine of Host Society:** Food habits of all the migrants may not be similar even if they have migrated from the same place. Cultural, regional, and religious variations might be there even within a country. Therefore, the adoption of food habits and developing taste for the cuisine of the host society by the migrants would vary from situation to situation. Some migrants will be more willing to adopt the food habits of the host society but there might be others who may resist. Reasons for such insulation could be different. Differences can also be observed between the first generation migrants and those who either came as kids or were born and brought up in the host society. The attitude of females in this connection may be more rigid and conservative. Since males have to interact more with the members of the host society, they may be less rigid. They may make some kind of adjustment due to the exigency of the situation, and thus the chances of becoming sandwiched between the two cultures are greater among men.

There are few dishes and food items which no more belong to one culture or society as they have been adopted universally, irrespective of the country of origin. For instance, Italian Pizza and American burgers have become part of dietary habits in many parts of the world. Similarly, some of the Indian dishes, both vegetarian (such as Dausa) and nonvegetarian (such as Tandoori Chicken), are relished by many people all over the world.

Insulatory Mechnisms

There are a number of insulatory mechanisms that may impede the process of assimilation. Immigrants with more insulatory mechanisms will be less prone to assimilation and will have more chances of being sandwiched between the host culture and the parent culture. The areas where apertures can be opened also serve as insulators if they are not allowed to be opened. Their operation, however, varies from society to society. In this section we briefly elaborate some of the prominent insulatory mechanisms.

(i) Retention of Mother Tongue

Immigrants adopt various means and ways to keep their mother tongue alive in a foreign land. There is a tendency amongst the immigrants to communicate with each other in their native language. At home, they generally use the native language and at the place of work the language of the host society. The larger the size of the immigrant group the greater is the chances of the mother tongue to survive or co-exist with the language of the host society. However, children have better capability of learning new languages, and they become fluent users of the language of the area where they are being brought up. Religious congregations and functions help promote the use of the parent language. Sometimes immigrants make special arrangements to teach native language to younger generation. Thus, members of the sandwich culture are likely to be bilingual. Migrants from the Latin America to USA offer a good example of this phenomenon. Most of these migrants converse only in Spanish; consequently, Spanish is emerging as a second language in the US, making the country bilingual. Same is the case with Chinese.

(ii) Concentration of Living Quarters to Promote Greater Interaction with the Members of the Group

Lodging in an entirely new environment especially when immigrants do not know the language of the host society may create problems of adjustments for new arrivals. In order to find a familiar environment, which may not be totally alien, immigrants prefer to settle initially in those areas where they may have some people from their own country. This facilitates their adjustment at new place and also keeps alive their own culture. When Indians in large number were taken as indentured labour by the British to distant lands, they were put together in separate barracks with little or no interaction with the local people. This facilitated their better integration as a migrant group and created a distance between them and the locals. A separate colony of immigrants served as a good insulator. One implication of concentration of immigrants at one place is that it reminds them about their parent culture and reduces their chances of full integration with the local community—in the sense that their identity does not get obliterated. Fiji Indians offer a good example of this phenomenon.

(iii) **Provision of Separate Educational Facilities for the Children**

Differences in the language of the host society and that of the migrants may create problems of schooling for the children of migrants especially when the medium of instruction is the language of the host society. In such cases, the migrants are left with two choices: either they send their children back home for schooling, or alternatively, run their own schools. Opening of schools at the place of migration may not be an easy option as it requires lot of efforts including finances and availability of teachers. Those migrants who are unable to use the facilities of schooling in the host society send their children back home. This ensures that children are initially kept away from a foreign culture and, at the same time remain in touch with their parent culture. But there might be many migrant groups who may open their own schools. Provision of separate educational facilities for immigrant children ensures their continuous exposure to the parent culture. This reduces, however, the chances of integration of immigrants into the culture of the host society. By providing educational facilities to their children, the immigrants teach not only the language but also encourage children to learn other aspects of their parent culture.

(iv) **Practice of Endogamy**

Endogamy is the characteristic feature of almost all societies though its intensity of application may vary from society to society. In traditional societies, it is practiced more rigidly. Indians who migrate to other countries, prefer, by and large, to select a spouse not only from India but also from the same religion and caste. Failing that, they may look for spouse in the country of their settlement preferably from the same religion and caste. Second generation migrants may adopt more liberal attitude while selecting a spouse. They may not hesitate marrying a person who may belong to a different caste but also to a different cultural region within their parent society. Inter-religious and inter-racial marriages especially with the people of host society, on the other hand, weaken the endogamous insulator.

(v) **Formation of Voluntary Organizations**

Formation of voluntary organizations by immigrants in a foreign country not only provides an opportunity for social gathering but also plays a significant role in keeping the parent culture alive. These voluntary organizations may be formed on the basis of religion, region, language or caste. Besides, there might be an organization which may provide opportunities to various groups from the same country living abroad to come in contact and to renew their affiliation with the parent culture.

(vi) **Concentration in Certain Occupations**

Traditionally, each caste in India has been assigned a specific occupation to be carried out, but now this has become redundant, as several vocational options are open for competition. But still there are few occupations which are carried out by people of a particular caste. But in a foreign country, the best candidates get the job, irrespective of their religion and caste. Indians in foreign countries are also opting for all kinds of jobs. Even Indians, who were imported as indentured labourers could not keep their caste intact, forget about the occupation. While travelling from India to various British colonies they spent many days in ship and in the process they lived together and also dined together. Upon reaching their destination, all of them were employed as labourers irrespective of their religion and caste. There are few occupations, such as those of priest in a temple, which go by caste otherwise caste based occupations are rarely followed in an alien society.

(vii) Pursuit of Parental Religion

Besides pursuing their own religious rituals at home immigrants also form various religious organizations and build their own temples of worship. These organizations celebrate various religious functions, which provide them an opportunity to interact with each other and expose younger generation to their religion and the parent culture.

(viii) Continuation of Food Habits and Taboos Associated with Eating

Old habits diehard. Food habits are no exception. All immigrants, irrespective of their place of settlement look for their familiar food dishes. Indians settled in foreign countries also generally prefer Indian food, occasional tasting of foreign food notwithstanding. There might be various reasons for not liking the food of the host society. Some immigrants from India continue with their choice of a particular kind of food though they may allow their children to eat food of their choice including non-vegetarian dishes. It is also possible that at home only vegetarian food is cooked but members might eat non-vegetarian food outside, thus observing a double standard.

Considerations of Purity and Pollution can be other factors. As some immigrants, especially Brahmans, may not eat food cooked by a person belonging to a particular caste or a different religion. Various kinds of food taboos are also observed by Indians. For instance, some Hindus avoid beef, and Muslims avoid Pork. Observing such taboos serve to insulate people from other non-membership groups.

(ix) Retention of Cultural Diacriticals

Continuation of cultural diacriticals, including dress, by immigrants may act as a deterrent in their integration. All immigrants prefer to wear their national dress especially on certain occasions; this is truer of women. Sikh gentlemen, irrespective of the fact whether they are in USA, or South Africa, or Thailand always wear turban and Kara (steel bangle) on wrist. Though some Sikh gentlemen in foreign countries have started keeping short hair but majority of them keep their beard intact. When these people visit India they always wear turban on their short hair. Similarly, some Pandits in Bangkok wear their traditional dress of Dhoti and Kurta and also put tilak on their forehead. Such visible diacritical marks can be seen among many immigrants in most of the countries. Indian women prefer to wear salwar kameez or saree but at work they may wear Jeans or other western dress.

(x) **Racial Features**

Racial features help differentiate people easily. In some countries inter-racial marriages do take place but such cases are not too many. Although so much racial miscegenation has already taken place that one cannot talk of pure race any more, prominent racial features are still to be seen such as Mongoloid character amongst the Chinese, and Negroid characters amongst most of the people from Africa. The case of Obama, present President of the United States, is a good example of a mixed marriage; he is described as "black". When interracial marriages occur they break this insulation and create conditions for the emergence of a sandwich culture.

(xi) **Contact with Parent Culture**

Keeping apertures open to the parent culture also serves as an insulator *vis-à-vis* the host culture. The greater the frequency of interaction with the parent culture the stronger is the bond with it. Such an inward orientation mars the prospects of identifying with the host community, and makes the migrant group a marginalized entity. The links with the parent culture are maintained, in several ways. Some of those are listed below:

(a) Frequent visits to homeland

Majority of the immigrants do not severe their relations with the people back home. Initially, the immigrants regularly visit their home town or invite family members to visit them. Visits to home country is one way by which immigrants are able to expose their children, who have been born and brought up in a foreign country, to their parent culture. Some immigrants may have immovable property in their home country and this requires regular visits to maintain them. Chances of such people to integrate and assimilate in the host society are relatively less.

(b) Schooling

When immigrants are not satisfied with the schooling facilities for their wards in the country of their migration they send their children back home. This happened with many Indian immigrants in Thailand who sent their children for education to India. One effect of sending children back home for education is that they escape early exposure to a foreign culture.

(c) Affinal and consanguineal relations

Affinal and consanguineal relations left behind affect the integration process. In rare cases, the entire family migrates. The kinsmen left behind serve not only as a reminder to the link in the country of origin, they extend all possible help to the émigrés in regard to mate selection, organization of family events, property matters, and a myriad other things. Such help cements the relationship and makes the migrants somewhat ambivalent in regard to a total curtailment of ties with the parent culture.

(d) Exposure to media, music, books and films

Music, books and films from one's parent country provide a much needed communication link. Through them, the migrants develop empathy with the parent culture and remain in touch with the latest developments in thinking, politics, and literature. Such links do not allow an easy breakdown of ties with one's own cultural milieu. They help in recreating the parent culture in an alien setting. Viewing the social and cultural programme through satellite one can always remain in touch with the parent culture.

(e) Postal and Telecommunication

Revolution in information technology has made communication so easy that now through e-mails one can instantly connect with any one in any part of the world. Developments in transnational network have allowed the immigrants to build social, cultural and marital relations in any part of the world. These developments have somewhat reduced the chances of assimilation of an immigrant group in the host society.

While analyzing the dynamics of apertures and insulatory mechanisms one has to keep in mind that all immigrants, even though originating from the same country, do not constitute a homogeneous group. The adaptation pattern depends on the socio-demographic characteristics of the migrants—differences in age, sex, education, religion, region, language, rural-urban background and so on. The conditions under which they have migrated may also differ and these may also affect their adaptation process. Even the attitude of the immigrants towards the members of the host society influences the adaptation process.

Cultural, contextual, and situational conditions of the immigrants determine the extent to which immigrants succeed in creating apertures to relate with, or in insulating themselves from, the host society. The cultural factors refer to the conditions in the parent society from where immigrants migrate and to the circumstances under which migration takes place. The contextual conditions are those which immigrants face in the host society. The experiences of individuals and groups in the host society may be referred to as situational conditions. These conditions differ from group to group and from country to country. Whether the immigrants are sandwiched between the parent culture and the host society, or are moving towards assimilation, would depend on these conditions.

III

The focus of this study is to analyse the various factors that have affected the process of integration of Indians immigrants in different countries. We may briefly outline these factors here.

I. Cultural Conditions

Cultural conditions include (a) social, economic and political conditions of the society, (b) motivation for migration, (c) demographic characteristics of the migrants, (d) attitude of the migrants towards members of the host society, (e) culture and religion of the immigrants, and (f) other social factors.

(a) Social, economic and political conditions of the parent society

To the extent migration is encouraged by the prevailing socio-economic and political conditions within the country of origin it is important to know under what conditions migration has taken place. Whether people had migrated on their own volition or whether they were forced by economic and political conditions, or by natural or man-made disasters. Indian emigration in ancient period was mainly cultural and commercial. At that time, migrants acted as cultural ambassadors of the great Hindu civilization and religion. Later, under the colonial regime, emigration took place mainly due to economic reasons, or due to the desire to visit the country of the colonial masters for purposes of study or service. In recent years, people migrate to other countries for a variety of other reasons, and they choose different destinations located in various continents of the world. There would be hardly any country in the world where people of Indian origin have not gone and settled.

Natural or man-made disasters also force people to migrate. Natural disasters include earthquakes, floods, or droughts. Man-made disasters are caused by internecine wars, or terrorism, or some other catastrophe caused by misuse of technology. Population groups that are rushed to reside in another country or territory are usually termed as refugees. The problems of refugees, and their adjustment with, or assimilation into the host society are different from the migrants. A significant difference is between those who seek temporary refuge, and look forward to resettlement back in their own country, and those who do not wish to return to their homeland.

In the case of an individual, or a single family migration the migrants are self-motivated to migrate and make good of their sojourn in a strange land. Such migration may also be of temporary character, or the one with a view to finally settling down. Temporary migrants may also change their decision and finally opt for a permanent settlement. Such a change happens when the migrating group finds the circumstances favourable; or when it perceives the situation back home as un-inviting.

(b) Motivation for migration

The motivation for migration may also affect the adaptation process. If people have migrated to earn and then return to the country of their origin, the chances are that such people will never try to adopt the culture of the host society. This was true for most of the early migrants from India. However, if the migrants move with the intention of staying permanently, the chances of their creating more apertures are quite high.

(c) Demographic characteristics of the migrants

Age, sex, education, religion, region, language, rural and urban background, and professional training are some of the characteristics which affect the status of migrants in an alien society. The acceptability of immigrants by the people of host society may depend upon these factors. If the immigrants are in a position to contribute to the development of the host society it would facilitate their settlement at the new place. But if the immigrants are seen as depriving the host people of their rights and opportunities they may face many problems as happened with Indians when they migrated to Canada in the beginning of the twentieth century. However, those who migrated to that country after 1960s did not face much problems.

(d) Attitude of migrants towards members of the host society

Attitude of migrants towards the members of the host society may influence the process of adaptation. If the migrants have pre-conceived unfavourable ideas about the host society they would not open out and remain confined in terms of their interactions with their own group members and with their people back at home.

(e) Culture and religion of the immigrants

Major differences in the culture and religion of the immigrants and of the members of the host society may mar interactions between the two sets of people.

(f) Other social factors

There are a number of other social factors which may deter the migrants to have more intimate interactions with the members of the host society.

II. Contextual Conditions

The contextual conditions refer to the conditions the migrants face in the host society. It may include social, economic and political conditions and attitude of the members of the host society towards migrants in general and towards a migrant group in particular.

(a) Social, economic and political conditions in the host society

When people migrate on their own, the destination is decided by them. In most cases, people decide about the destination where the economic conditions are favourable. Sometimes the policies of the host society do not allow migrants to settle permanently. The countries of the Middle East and Gulf fall in this category. People who temporarily migrate to these countries, go with the sole intention of making some money and then return to their base. It is also possible that the countries of migration may allow limited entries and also limit the period of their sojourn. Therefore, it becomes imperative for the migrants to take into account the social and political conditions of the host society, in addition to economic considerations. Since the conditions are comparatively more favourable in Western countries especially in Canada, U.S.A. and U.K., most of the migrants from developing countries give preference to these countries. In the last few years, the trend of Indians migrating to Australia and to New Zealand is also rising.

When highly trained professionals from the less developed countries migrate to developed countries for better quality of life, the process is called Brain Drain. Depending on the absorptive capacity of the economy and the quality of working life, Atal and Dall'Oglio (1987)[2] identified four types of countries as follows:

Type A: Countries with absorptive capacity and a healthy work environment.

Type B: Countries with absorptive capacity but poor work environment.

Type C: Countries with no absorptive capacity but healthy work environment.

Type D: Countries low on both the scores.

According to Atal and Dall'Oglio[3] Type A countries should face no problem of Brain Drain. In fact, these countries are the labour receiving countries. Emigration occurring from countries of C and D cannot be called Brain Drain as they do not possess the absorptive capacity, argue the authors. Such countries may even encourage emigration. Till few years back India was one of the countries from where many professionals migrated to developed countries. However, globalization and liberalization in the last few years have altered the situation to some extent.

(b) Attitude of the host society towards migrants in general and towards a particular migrant group

The biased attitude of the members of the host society towards migrants may act as an insulator. Sometimes, preference may be given to a particular group. A comparison between the European immigrants and the migrants from Asian countries to USA and Canada, or Australia and New Zealand exemplifies this point.

III. Situational Conditions

Third set of conditions are related with the individual experiences of the immigrants, and institutional and associational facilities available to the immigrants in the host society which may affect the nature of Sandwich Culture.

(a) Individual experiences

Individual experiences of migrants may differ. The experience of their encounters with the members of the host society may affect their decision whether to settle there or to return. The immigrants might have to go through the process of enculturation to facilitate their adjustment. For instance, people who migrate to Thailand, must learn Thai language if they want to live and work in Thailand. Therefore, Indian migrants first stay with their friends or kinsmen for enculturation. In the process, they learn the language and also familiarize themselves with the culture of the host society.

(b) Institutional and associational facilities

Almost all migrants establish their own religious, educational and cultural institutions and also form their associations which may be based on religion, region and language and caste. These institutions and associations play significant role in exposing the younger people to their parent culture. They also provide an opportunity to the migrants to meet each other. Greater interactions between the immigrants may help develop better solidarity and maintain a separate identity, thus serving as a partial insulation to exposure to the majority community.

(c) Length of stay in the host society

Length of stay in the host society affects the process of adjustment. Generally, the first generation migrants find it difficult to integrate, but the process may start with the second and third generation, especially by those who are born and brought up in the new society.

IV

Objectives of the Study

Although the Sandwich culture phenomenon is universal and is applicable to Diaspora from other countries as well, this study is confined only to Indian Migrants (diaspora) and the theory of Sandwich culture is tested only for this limited sample.

The studies of Indian Diaspora have been undertaken with varied objectives and different perspectives. There is a need to review these studies and systematically present the findings. In this study, attempt has been made to present such a synthesis. This has been done by re-examining the existing studies with a view to answering the following questions:

1. How people with different socio-economic backgrounds, and hailing from different regions of the Indian sub-continent, have adjusted and adapted to the new environment? How the "cultural" factors have affected their adaptation process?
2. Have the Indian migrants integrated and assimilated in the host society? Or are they Sandwiched between the two cultures? An attempt has been made in this study to find out the functioning of apertures and insulators in different cultural contexts.

3. How the conditions in the host society and the situational factors have affected culture of immigrants?

The theory of Sandwich Culture hypothesizes that larger the number of apertures created by the migrants, the better are their chances of integration and assimilation in the host society. The migrants who adopt more insulatory mechanisms reduce their chances of assimilation in the host society. Such migrants will be more prone to be sandwiched between the two cultures.

Some other hypotheses tested in this study are:

(a) The elements of the host society which have bearing on day-to-day activities find easy acceptance by the migrant group such (e.g. language).

(b) Intermarriages between the members of the host society and the migrants enhance the chances of assimilation.

(c) Migrants who maintain continuous contact with people back home have lesser chances of assimilation.

(d) Migrants who form their own associations, run educational institutions and religious organizations, have lesser chances of assimilation.

(e) The lower the socio-economic status of the migrants, the higher are chances of insulatory mechanisms in operation.

(f) Third and fourth generation migrants create more apertures and have better chances of assimilation.

(g) Migrants who do not encounter discriminatory behaviour and prejudiced attitude from the members of the host society are more prone to assimilation.

(h) Migrants who do not compete for economic and political power with the members of the host society have more chances of assimilation.

The Methodology

To answer the above set of questions and to test the proposed hypotheses the data have been culled out from the available studies. Quite a few studies of Indian migrants in different countries by Indian as well as by foreign scholars are available. Some of these studies are of indentured labour settled in distant places such as Fiji in the Pacific, and Trinidad and

Guyana in the Caribbean. These people were transported by the British during colonial period and they have now settled in these countries. Quite a few studies of Indians settled in countries of the West especially in U.S.A., and Britain, who migrated on their own either to pursue higher studies or to seek gainful employment have been conducted. Few studies of Indians settled in the neighbouring countries of South Asia and South-east Asia such as Thailand, Singapore and Malaysia are also available. One study of Indians in Middle East (*Middle East Inerlude: Asian Workers Abroad* edited by Manolo I. Abella and Yogesh Atal (1986) is available but it was a study of those who have returned.

Since it is not possible to consider all the studies of Indian Diaspora in one volume, it has been decided to restrict this study to a few countries. The countries included in this study are the United States of America, Trinidad, and Thailand.

The data from these studies have been culled out on the following aspects:

1. The cultural aspects of the host society such as language, food habits, etc. adopted by the immigrants.
2. Inter-marriages between the members of the host society and the immigrants.
3. The activities of the religious, educational and other voluntary organizations of the immigrants.
4. Economic and political activities of the immigrants.
5. Nature of contact maintained with the parent culture in the form of (i) frequent visits, (ii) exposure to media such as films, music, books, etc., and (iii) affinal relations.
6. Attitude of the host society towards migrants and *vice-versa*.

The attempt is to find out the stages of assimilation and types of Sandwich Cultures developed by the Indian communities in the countries of their migration. An attempt has also been made to identify the factors which facilitate integration or hinder the process of assimilation and integration of immigrants in the host society.

CHAPTER-2

Trinidadian Indians

The history of Indian migration to distant lands is old and varied. Pre-colonial migration, however was voluntary. Migration during colonial period was somewhat varied. One important feature of migration during this period was in the form of "indentured" labour.[4] It was the "practice of binding individual workers to a set term of service in a specific country for any employer who would purchase his or her contract of indenture". The first set of indentured labour were the British people who migrated to North America soon after the abolition of slavery. In the 19th and early 20th centuries Asian workers were recruited as indentured labour for employment in European colonial empires in the Caribbean and the Asia-Pacific region. Indentured labour was widely used to transport workers from India for employment on sugar plantations in the Caribbean from 1839. Indians also went as indentured labour to Fiji in the Pacific, and to Malaysian plantations. Reports suggest that the conditions for indentured workers were usually very poor. Many died during the passage because they were huddled up in a small ship with limited facilities. During the term of indenture, the worker was not allowed to change employer, although the employer could sell the remaining period of indenture, a practice reminiscent of slavery. The Indians gave this system the name of *Girmitiya*—a strange concoction of the phrase government permit, used for indenture.[5]

Trinidad became an independent country in 1962 after 165 years of British rule. Indian migration to Trinidad began in 1845 with the withdrawal of African labour from plantation work and continued up to 1917, except for a short period between 1848 and 1851 when no one was transported. African slaves were imported by British after they took over the colony from Spain in 1797, to work on sugar plantations, which is the core of Trinidad economy. Though slavery was abolished in 1807, the African slaves continued as regular and full-time plantation labour until their emancipation from slavery, in 1838. Some of the African slaves occupied vacant land that was available in good quantity in Trinidad. Few purchased privately hold land. A handful of them went to towns and became artisans, petty traders, and stevedores.[6]

The withdrawal of African labour from plantation work led to crisis situation. The planters had no funds to make technological changes. They were not ready to deal with ex-slaves as free workers. It was, therefore, decided to import cheap and easily managed labour force. After trying labour force from many countries including China, the British authorities settled for labour from India as they were found to be the most efficient. Since India was also under British control they were no legal hurdles in the transportation of labour from India to Trinidad.

A total of 144,000 Indians were brought as labourers to Trinidad between 1845 and 1917. About 90 per cent of the migrants came from the provinces of North mainly from the then United Provinces and Oudh[7] (both are now part of Uttar Pradesh, retaining the same acronym, i.e. U.P. which was earlier an abbreviation for United Provinces), Bihar, Orissa and the Central Provinces (now part of Madhya Pradesh). The rest of the immigrants were from Bengal, the North-West Provinces (now part of Pakistan), and from the South. Hindi was the predominant language of the immigrants. Though people of all castes, including Brahmans and Rajputs, migrated to Trinidad, they were outnumbered by people of low castes and by people who hailed from the middle ranks of the Hindu caste hierarchy. Around 1880s, the caste composition in Trinidad was: "Brahman and other high castes 18 per cent; artisan castes 8.5 per cent, agricultural castes 32 per cent, low castes 41.5 per cent" (Brereton, 1974: 26).

The workers agreed to migrate to the remote colonies because of the economic crisis. Before industrial revolution, the British markets had demand for Indian handicrafts. After Industrial Revolution, the decision of the British government to restrict the import of Indian goods rendered thousands of Indians unemployed. With the imposition of high land tax the conditions of the farmers became precarious. Frequent famines in Bengal and North India added to the misery. Caste factor prevented people to accept jobs other than allowed by custom. Since there were no large-scale industries in the country, the miserable economic conditions of the poor farmers forced them to accept the job of labourers in remote colonies.

II

Trinidad is a heterogeneous society with Negroes and Indians as two major groups. In 1963, according to the Annual *Statistical Digest* (No. 13) of Trinidad and Tobago, Negroes constituted 43 per cent of the total population followed by 36 per cent Indians. Seventeen per cent of the total population of Trinidad was of mixed race, whereas only two per cent were Whites. The White population included the descendants of French, Scottish, Irish and Flemish immigrants. There was a small percentage of Portuguese and Chinese also. By 1980, out of a total population of 1,055,763 the population of Indians and Africans became more or less identical (Indians 40.7 per cent and Africans 40.8 per cent). The number of mixed people came down to 16.3 per cent and that of Whites was reduced to 0.9 per cent. Religion-wise distribution of population of Trinidad is Roman Catholics 38 per cent, Hindus 23 per cent, Anglicans 21 per cent, Muslims 6 per cent and other groups 12 per cent. Though people of various religious faith have migrated to Trinidad but in this study I have mainly concentrated on Hindus only.

Indians differed from other groups not only in their value orientation and beliefs but also in their customs and traditions such as marriage, family, kinship, religion, festivals as well as in dance and music. Initially, they could not perseverate their culture and customs but once they were free from indentured contract they succeeded in rebuilding their key institutions and at the same time accepted some socio-cultural elements of other groups. Rebuilding of their traditional customs and revival of their culture was facilitated due to their numerical preponderance. It gained momentum after India became an independent country. This was the period when Indians opened schools and also started building religious places. Youth clubs and study groups were also formed to revive cultural pride of Indians. The process was further enhanced by the screening of Indian movies. People thronged to watch these movies though they were unable to understand the dialogues which were in Hindi, even then they thought that Indian movies reminded them of their parent culture. Indian cultural troupes who performed in Trinidad also helped in renewing their link with India as large number of Indians including women attended such functions. In the beginning, caste did not affect the social relations but with the revival of customs people became conscious of their caste status. The Brahmans who occupied higher status, looked down upon low caste Chamar. Similarly Indians from North-West region looked down upon people from South India.

Residential Pattern of Indians

Distribution of population according to area and ethnicity shows that there are few pockets where Indians have outnumbered Africans. More than 86 per cent of the population of San Fernando in 1977 was of Indian origin. In Caroni, the percentage of Indians is more than 78. The Indian population of around 70 per cent in Victoria and more than 63 per cent in St. Patrick are other areas where Indians have concentrated. With around two per cent of Indian population, Tobago has the lowest number of Indians. In St. David also Indian population is less than ten per cent (Nikongo, 1994).

Indians came to Trinidad as agricultural labourers under contract to work on sugar, and later on cocoa plantations for a minimum of five years. They were entitled until 1895 to a free return passage to India if they remained for another five years. After the expiry of this period they were allowed to take whatever savings they had accumulated. Since Indians were quite efficient and hard working, the planters wanted them to continue even after the expiry of their contract. To retain them, the planters offered a few acres of crown land, if they gave up their claim to return passage to India. It was done with the hope that Indians would settle around the plantations and would work for them on part-time basis especially during the crop season besides cultivating their small plots of land. In order to attract them, changes were made in the employment policy, and the crown land was allowed to be purchased by the persons of small means.

No attempt was made by Indians to develop social relations with the locals as they had no ambition to settle permanently in Trinidad. The contract was designed in such a way that their chances of developing social contact with other groups were limited. They were not even allowed to leave the plantation without an official pass from the plantation authorities, and if caught without pass they were imprisoned. Indians were mainly concentrated in the sugar belt and were surrounded by other Indians. Their contact with the locals was restricted to their visits to towns for legal work. Besides language barrier, culturally also they were miles apart. The conditions under which they lived, have been called as "peaceful coexistence" rather than "peaceful coactivity" (Bahadoorsingh, 1968). The mutual prejudices between Indians and Negroes did not allow them to create apertures. The negative feelings by Indians and Negroes towards each other reduced their chances of any aperture openings with the result that they insulated from each other.

Vocational Activities of Indians

Indians were brought as indentured labour to Trinidad to work in sugar plantations. They were called "coolies"—a derogatory term used in India for the labourer hired to load and unload baggage. Since agricultural labourers belonged to the lower strata of the Trinidad society, Indians were placed in that category. Indians were also branded as "Pagans" or "heathens", because they were non-Christians and inferior. After the arrival of Indians, Africans shifted from sugar plantations to cocoa plantations, which were financially more lucrative. As a consequence, many uneducated black men became prosperous. With the growth of island economy, communication and transport network also improved. Many Negroes from the countryside migrated to towns to engage in secondary occupations. Since these occupations were regarded as more respectable, Negroes preferred these jobs despite poor salaries. They took advantage of converting to Christianity; their exposure to education by Churches gave them additional leverage. The most prestigious occupations were those connected with the ownership and management of estates, large commercial establishments, or with the upper notch of the civil services. By keeping themselves on plantations and not educating their children, Indians remained outside the main stream of the Trinidad society.

With the expiry of indenture contract Indians shifted to other vocations. This facilitated re-emergence of castes especially in rural Trinidad. There were some Indians who went back to their traditional occupation: "...the kumhar (potter) took to pottery, nai (barber) to his traditional work, teli (oil-processor) to his own, some Brahmans to teaching and priesthood, bania (grocer) to grocery, and ahir or goala to cattle rearing as well as milk-selling and the lowest castes to scavenging. The mallah took to fish and crab catching and the chamar would beat drums at festivals" (Jha, 1974: 11). Some high caste people, like Rajputs, became landlords. The migrants from Bihar who belonged to Kori, Kurmi and Kahar castes took to cultivation.

Differences in ethnic groups are also reflected in economic and occupational divisions. Big industrial units, as well as large commercial banks, are mostly controlled by White people—British and Americans. Majority of the jobs in civil, judicial, and police services are taken by Negroes. Indians, who mainly worked on sugar plantations, concentrated in rural areas and remained backward as they did not realize the importance of education. They did not send their children to schools as they were afraid of their getting converted to Christianity. Moreover, they wanted their children to help them in the fields to contribute to family income. But gradually they realized their mistake, and encouraged their children to go to schools. Since Indians were debarred from civil services they sought careers in business and other related professions such as transportation and entertainment

(Malik, 1971). Despite all these developments, Indians have remained largely backward compared to other groups.

Trinidad's attainment of independence from the British and the phenomenon of 'oil boom' (1973-82) brought significant changes in the ethnic division of labour as new avenues of economic opportunities in business, bureaucracy, and other professions emerged. Increase in the oil prices in the 1970s changed the economy of Trinidad. The government of Trinidad abandoned the five-year plans of development and opted for the industrial diversification with foreign investors as partners. The government favoured "...two petrochemical plants, a second ammonia factory, an aluminium smelter, an iron and steel works, additional fertilizer plants, and widespread electrical expansion" (Vertovec, 1990: 96). It was also decided to nationalize the major industrial sectors. To reduce unemployment the government expanded public works programmes and lowered taxes. Most of these developments were designed to help Negroes, at the cost of Indians. The boom affected manufacturing, construction, and transport industries, and the businessmen and entrepreneurs engaged in these professions prospered.

By adapting the capitalist development policy, the Trinidadian government protected the interests of upper and middle classes of both the ethnic groups, i.e. Indians and Africans. Most of the programmes adopted by the government of Eric Williams of People's National Movement (PNM) favoured the African working class. All this was done at the cost of agricultural development which declined substantially. The decline in agricultural production negatively affected the Indians who were mainly confined to rural areas. Despite the indifferent attitude of the government towards the Indian working class, Indians managed to benefit substantially, especially in construction and transportation sectors as these were not under government control.

The development programmes also changed the nature of employment in rural Trinidad, including the villages inhabited by the Indians. Due to higher wages in government sponsored projects people in rural areas preferred to work as labourers; but this shift to other vocations affected the cultivation of cane and rice. People could afford to buy rice from the market instead of growing it in their own fields. Large number of women also joined these projects which added to the family income. The perception of the villagers also changed. The younger generation of Indians who were better educated than their parents did not blindly follow the traditional ways of Indians. They preferred to identify themselves with the western pop culture. They did not like the traditional lifestyle of their parents and this led to sizeable generation gap. Many youths labelled them as 'old' time Indians or lowly 'coolies' (Vertovec, 1990: 103).

The slump in oil prices at the International level in 1981-82 adversely affected the economy in Trinidad. Most of the industries established during the boom period suffered losses and needed government support to survive. Unemployment increased as many people lost their jobs especially those who were employed in manufacturing, construction, and transportation sectors. Subsidies for domestic consumption provided by the government were cut down. This affected the working class including Indians to a large extent.

Caste among Indians in Trinidad

Questions have been raised regarding the legitimacy of the castes of Indians when they migrated to Trinidad as indentured labour. As no record of castes was maintained at the time of recruitment of labour some of the low caste people also declared themselves as of high caste as they hailed from different regions and no body could refute their claim. Majority of the Indians in Trinidad believe that a caste of a person can be recognized by his behaviour, his manners and his food habits. The major criteria to determine the position of a caste in terms of hierarchy depended on the presence, or absence, of practice of swine-raising and pork eating (Klass, 1961). Though caste identities re-emerged after indentured period was over, but "... no caste system ever arose to control or influence personal or group interaction" (Vertovec, 1994: 135).

Caste plays significant role in deciding social relations in India but the Indians who migrated as indentured labour could not keep their caste status intact in Trinidad. While travelling in ship for months, all of them were huddled together and shared accommodation and ate the same food without bothering about the caste of the cooks. After landing in Trinidad, all of them were classified as coolies and lived together in barracks. The "...life in the barracks or work on the field or in the factory hardly permitted the observance of caste segregation and untouchability or the ideas associated with purity and pollution" (Jayaram, 2006: 151). Other factors which weakened caste were imbalance in sex ratio, skewed age composition and proselytizing activities of the Canadian Mission. Since the number of females recruited as indentured labour was negligible, high caste males took low caste females as their partners ignoring caste factor as they were not willing to accept African women as their life partners. Majority of those who were hired as indentured labour were in the age group of 20-30 and did not know the working of caste factors. At the same time, Canadian Presbyterian Mission was actively pursuing Indians to convert to Christianity in lieu of financial benefits. All these factors led to the weakening of the caste (Jayaram, 2006).

Brahmans were able to re-establish their special status by resuming their priestly ritualistic functions. Hindu community badly needed the services of a Brahman on occasions of birth, marriage, and death. The role of a priest among Hindus is considered extremely important to provide psychological protection from a society basically hostile to them racially, culturally, and economically. "In the Hindu household or temple...the Pundit...would be the focus of social and cultural resistance, expounding from their wealth of religious literature—the Ramayana, the Bhagavat Gita, the Mahabharata—traditional Indian values and warning against conversion to Christianity" (Kelvin Singh, 1974: 49-50). The services of Brahman were used to perform worship including that of Hanuman and Satyanarayan, the samskaras (rites of passage), and yagnas and the recital of Bhagvata Purana. These functions were attended by large number of people. Some of these activities still continue but in modified form (Vertovec, 1994).

Family, Marriage and Kinship

Kinship relationships are indispensable to Indians. They carried this trait to Trinidad. They succeeded to restore the basic characteristics of their culture through social institutions such as family and kinship once they were free from indenture contract. High degree of unanimity in the use of kinship terminology among Indians has been found despite the fact that they hailed from different parts of India. Due respect is accorded to elderly persons and classificatory term of uncle and aunt are used to address them. The analysis of kinship terminology gives no indication of any major change. "Kinship is one of the most important structural relationships in the community, and it includes numerous real or supposed uncles, aunts, sisters and cousins, grandfather and grandmother—from both the mother's and the father's side. Each person is accorded a status in the kinship group hierarchy and receives his due respect. The Indian child is brought up under a complex structure of kinship relations and family authority patterns. He is taught to obey his elders, pay them respect, and share manifold family responsibilities" (Malik, 1971: 27).

Like kinship, family's role is seminal in the life of an individual even in a foreign country. Family plays a significant role in transmitting cultural values to their children. Indians from the beginning restricted the social interaction of their children with the Negro children. Thus they succeeded in insulating their children from outside world from the beginning and did not allow them to have any apertures in the host society. The only change found in the social structure of Indians in Trinidad is in the status of women, who enjoy more freedom as compared to their counterparts in India. This happened due to their exposure to higher education and westernization, especially in urban areas. However, their participation in public and political life is still restricted.

The oil boom of the 1970s affected the social and cultural institutions of Indians in Trinidad. Nuclear family became quite common. Girls got more freedom and were permitted to work outside the home or village. And yet people maintained relations with the members of their lineage. Family based rituals such as pujas, Ramayana readings and yagnas became more common than ever before. Young people with their newly achieved economic windfall increasingly sponsored these events for the welfare of their family and also to enhance their prestige. Earlier, family and community were the main agents of transmission of culture, but now besides family, it is also transmitted through schools and mass media.

It must, however, be said that interpersonal roles within the household have changed in the contemporary Trinidad. The parental authority based on traditional values has weakened as more and more young people take their own decisions even in regard to the selection of a spouse. Earlier Indians used to marry their wards between the ages of 12 to 14 but now the age for marriage varies between 16 and 30. The selection of the spouse for their wards was done earlier by the parents of both the parties after collecting all information including the family background. Once they were satisfied the date of marriage was fixed. Now even the role of girls have changed. Earlier the girls were confined to domestic work but now they are opting for jobs outside. This has given them more freedom in the selection of their life partners. Though divorce is legally possible but very few Indians opt for this. Instead of divorce, couple favour separation, the rate of which is very high (Nevadomsky, 1983).

Caste endogamy could not be maintained because of a severe shortage of women and in the process even the principle of gotra exogamy is ignored. At present, inter-caste marriages are rather common. But the marriages between a high caste girl and a low caste boy (hypogamy) are still not accepted. However hypergamous marriages are quite common (Klass, 1961; Jha, 1974; Nevadomsky, 1983). Arranged marriages and the parental consent which were mandatory earlier have been replaced by personal choice. Before 1946 marriages by Indian priests were not legally approved but now marriages performed by Hindu priests are allowed to be registered officially.

Besides inter-caste marriages, inter-religious marriages between Hindus and Muslims from India are also becoming popular especially among urban middle classes. Young people go ahead with such marriages even if it is not approved by the families of both the partners. In most of the cases such marriages are accepted as they think that the culture of such unions will be more Indian rather than Creole culture. Hindus, who were quite rigid even in the case of inter-caste marriages are becoming more flexible towards inter-religious marriages. Similarly, marriages between Hindus and the East Indian Christians, especially those of Hindu descent, are also taking place and gradually people are accepting such marriages (Malik, 1971). This is due to the fact that many converts to Christianity are Hindus and many of them still read and recite Hindu sacred books like the *Ramayanas* and the *Bhagwad Gita*.

Sharp differences in racial features of the Indians and the Negroes is the reason for disapproving marriages between the two groups by majority of the Indians. Hindus are strongly against marriages with Negroes but they approve such unions with White people. They think that marriages with White people will enhance their status. Cultural incompatibility is the main reason for disapproving marriages with Negroes as the Indian cultural values are completely different from the Creole culture. The children born of mixed marriages between the Negroes and the Indians are called *Dogala* (hybrid). Indians are also afraid that their marriages with Negroes would affect their Indian identity.

Indian Languages

Indian immigrants in Trinidad came from different parts of India and brought with them their own dialects such as Magadhi, Maithili, Bengali, Oriya, Assamese, Tamil, Telugu, Malayalam, Urdu and a few more. Since the major chunk of migrants have come from Uttar Pradesh and Bihar the dominant languages among Indians are Vrajbhasha (Paschmi Hindi), Awadhi (Purvi Hindi) and Bhojpuri. However, the Bhojpuri continues to be the most popular spoken language (Jha, 1974). One of these three dialects can still be found in the folk and ritual songs among Indians in Trinidad. The social conditions in Trinidad were such that Indians had to develop one language for communication amongst themselves and another to communicate with the authorities. To adopt a language for internal communication was not an easy task as they hailed from different parts of India. It was found that "even the Bhojpuri brought to Trinidad was not homogeneous, and it reflected the dialectal variations of the parts from which the speakers came. In due course, however, through a process of *Koineisation* (that is, levelling) of different dialects, a new variant of Bhojpuri was evolved as a reasonably homogenous *lingua franca* in the sugar plantations" (Jayaram, 2000: 44). Linguistis had called the new dialect as "Trinidad Bhojpuri"; also known as "Plantation Hindustani" (Vertovec, 1994, and Jayaram, 2000). Even Trinidad Bhojpuri could not become the language of the Indians as younger generation were more keen to adopt Creole English or standard English.

Indians constituted 40.3 per cent of the total population of Trinidad in 1990. There are organizations such as Bhartiya Vidya Sansthaan (established in 1966) and Hindi Nidhi (established in 1986). The Indian Council for Cultural Relations and the High Commission of India readily provide support and guidance to the promoters of Hindi. Hindi is also used in all religious functions. Audio-visual programmes also expose the Indian migrants to Hindi (Jayaram 2000). And yet Hindi could not be revived as it is seldom used in interpersonal communication in everyday life within the community. Even those who had learnt the language feel shy to use it. Younger generation of Indians, especially those living in urban areas, have adopted creole English and/or standard English.

Names of Indians

In the early days of their indentured period some Hindus adopted Christian names, for example, Krishna Deonarain changed his name to Adrian Cola Reinzi. There were others who angilicised their Hindu names such as Hari Lal became Harry and Kishan became Chris (Jayaram, 2003). But now the trend has changed. People are reverting to their original Hindu names but with change in their spellings and pronunciation. Low caste Indians—who migrated from Uttar Pradesh and Bihar—do not use any surname. Among the people from upper castes use of surnames is quite common; one comes across surnames like Misra (Mishra), Sukul (Shukla), Pandey, Dubey and Tiwari. Names of some pioneer emigrants like Gopal

(Gopaul) became the last part of the name of his descendants. "Some names of Indians in Trinidad, as in U.P. and Bihar, are even now connected with the name of the day on which a person was born such as Ravi (Sunday); Samaroo (from Somavar or Monday); Mangal or Mungal or Mungaloo or Mungaroo (from Tuesday); Budu or Budhoo or Boodoo (from Budha or Wednesday); Vrishaspati (Thursday); Sukra (Friday); and Sanichar (Saturday). In case of females, Sanichar becomes Sanichari and Mangal becomes Mangali" (Jha, 1974: 13). Names connected with Ram and Krishna are also very common, such as Ramaprasad, Ramanaresh, Ramabissoon, Rama Kissoon, Bissoondial, Bisoondath, Kissoondath, Deokissoon, Balkissoon, Srikissoon, Jaikissoon. Some people have names connected with Lord Shiva such as Bhola, Mahadeo, and Shambhoo. Among the females, names such as Sita, Tara, Radha, Parvati, Lakshmi or Lachhnin, Indra or Indrani and Gayatri are quite common. Names connected with sacred rivers of India as well as sacred places are also very common, such as Ganga, Yamuna, Mathura, Awadh, Pariyag and Kashi, etc. One can also find street names and also names connected with places and persons, such as Agra street, Ayodha street, Calcutta settlement, Fyzabad, Mathura street, Madras settlement, Benares street, Delhi street, Katwaroo trace, Mahess Road, Abdool village, Akal Road, Kalloo Road, Jogie Road, Pujadas street, etc. (*ibid.*: 13-14). All these names indicate the place of origin of Indian migrants. It appears that Indians in Trinidad continue to identify themselves with the region from where they have migrated.

Education among Indians

During the early phase of the indentured era Indians did not send their children to English education schools, as they were alarmed by the proselytizing activities of the Christian denominational schools. They did not want to alienate their children, and wanted to preserve their religious and cultural values. Some Indians were of the view that Western education would denigrate their social origin (Kelvin Singh, 1974). Moreover, children were important contributors to the family income and sending them to school meant withdrawing them from work and thus adversely affecting family economy. But by late 1940s and early 1950s they realized the significance of education and took steps to set up schools of their own denomination and hired Indian teachers. The lead to open schools was taken by *Sanatan Dharam Maha Sabha*. Most of these schools were opened in the areas mainly inhabited by Indians. The school exposed the children to Indian epics like *Mahabharat* and *Ramayan* and to other aspects of Hindu religion. Arrangements for teaching Hindi to their children were also made in temples. Youth clubs and study groups were also formed which also contributed in the revival of mother tongue.

Food

Indian migrants to other countries generally prefer their own food. Indians in Trinidad are no exception. Since majority of them in Trinidad came from Uttar Pradesh and Bihar they continued to have their traditional food of *roti, rice, dal* (split beans) and vegetables along with *chatni*, and *achar* (pickle). The favourite vegetables include *jhingi*, *karaili* and *sahijan*. There are few dishes such as karhi, dalpuri, khir (rice pudding), dahi (yogurt), and a few vegetables like potato, brinjal (eggplant or aubergine), radish, squash (*lauki*) which are considered special. Some Indian sweets like *laddu*, *jalebi* and *gulab-jamun* are also available in the market. Indian style cooking has been further facilitated due to availability of spices used in Indian cuisine (Jha, 1974). The social and physical conditions under which Indians were transported to Trinidad broke caste and religion based rules of commensality. So was the case with vegetarianism. In Trinidad "curry" is made with curry powder and not by mixing a curry paste. The prevalence of "curry" in Trinidadian food resembles to some extent to certain varieties of Indian food. It has been noticed that curry is as much a part of Trinidadian food as of Indian food. Another item which has become a part of Trinidadian food is *chutney*, which is again of Indian origin. There are few dishes in Trinidad which can be compared with Indian dishes: "...saheena is like pakoras, "doubles" is a variation of the channa batura, though more in the form of chick-peas sandwich, and their kachowrie has a marked similarity to its namesake in India".[8] The main meals of people in Trinidad which includes goat curry (mutton) and roti is again of Indian origin. However, majority of the Indians in Trinidad still prefer roti, dal and vegetable in all the three meals—breakfast, lunch, and dinner.

Music of Indians

Initially the source of entertainment of Indians was their music, dance and drama which they brought with them to Trinidad. Though classical music in Trinidad has disappeared but the folk music in the form of *Hori*, *Jhumar*, *Dhrupad*, and *Basant* are still sung at the time of holi—the festival of colour. On special occasions *Thumri* and *gazal* are also sung. Before the advent of Indian films and songs in Trinidad, the traditional dance dramas like *Ramleela*, *Krishnaleela* and *Rasmandal*, *Indrasabha*, *Raja Harishchandra* were quite popular. But now most of these traditional dance and dramas have been replaced by Indian films and their songs. Some of the traditional musical instruments like *sarangi*, *sitar*, *dholak*, *tabla*, and *harmonium* are still quite popular (Jha, 1974: 10). Some local singers copy the voice of popular singers from Bollywood and entertain the crowd by singing popular Indian film songs. The impact of oil boom in seventies also enhanced popularity of Indian film songs as people could afford to buy stereos and videos of Hindi films. All these developments brought Indians closer to their parent culture.[9]

A new form of music called *chutney* which is a mixture of Indian and Trinidad music has been created by the younger generation of Indians. *Chutney* music has become quite popular not only in Trinidad but in some Western countries like USA, UK, and Canada. Some Indians have specialised in singing Calypso which is the national music of Trinidad and exclusive preserve of Afro-Trinidadians. Indians have also adopted the steel band of Negroes and some Indians became famous player of this band. "But it was in the creation of chutney songs and rhythms that Indians found their own Soca or soul music. Taking with easy abandon rhythms from pan and rap, and drawing from the well-springs of Indian folk and even more so film music, Indians evolved a distinct musical form. ...the prevalence of Hindi words in chutney helped to maintain a living contact between Indo-Trinidadians and those they left behind in India" (Manas, 2009: 3). Chutney music is best example of sandwich culture.

Diacritical Identification of Indians

All groups and communities have certain diacritical cultural identification marks which distinguish them from other groups. There may not be much difference in the dress of men but this is not so for females. Most Indian women wear sarees even when they migrate to other countries. Older women in Trinidad still stick to their saree though younger females have started wearing Western dress including jeans and skirt. The young females also wear salwar and kameez. But on special occasions saree is generally preferred. Indian males also wear traditional dress of dhoti-kurta or payjama-kurta on special festive occasions. There are some special shops in certain parts of Trinidad where Indian goods including clothes are available (Jha, 1974 and Jayaram, 2003).

Religion and Festivals

Indians who came to Trinidad as indentured labour hailed from different parts of the country. It is possible that in the initial stages some Indians might have tried to pursue their traditional religious practices related to regional, village, caste or kin group gods. But after putting up together for a long period they might have discontinued their parochial practices. Among the various groups, the presence of Ramanandis, Kabir Panthis, Aghoris and Shivnarayanis has been recorded by the end of 19th century. Gradually, they started constructing rudimentary form of temples for worship which were modified later on leading to the proliferation of temples. This was followed by the celebrations of various Hindu festivals like Holi and Diwali.

It was from 1860 onwards that Hindus in Trinidad started celebrating their festivals in a big way when Hindu temples were built and priests were engaged. Though Indian migrants brought almost all the ritualistic traditions of Uttar Pradesh, and Bihar with them, they pursued their religious practices modestly. The celebrations began with Shiva-ratri, Phagwa (Hori or Holi), Ramleela and Divali (Jha, 1974). Majority of the Hindus in Trinidad have retained their faith and belief in the triad of Gods namely Brahma (The creator), Vishnu (the preserver), and Mahesh (the destroyer) The most popular festivals of the Hindus in Trinidad are Diwali and Holi. On Diwali day, Hindus decorate their houses and illuminate their places of business. "On the occasion of Divali, Lakshmi the Goddess of wealth, is worshipped in many Hindu homes: the image of the goddess is washed in milk or water, Prasad (offering) offered and bhajan (devotional songs) sung in her honour" (Jha, 1974: 8). Another important festival celebrated by Hindus in Trinidad is the festival of Holi. "The Hori or Kabira songs sung to the accompaniment of dholak (small drum), Jhal or Majira and sometime Harmonium, are the same as those brought from U.P and West Bihar...The Chowtal singing competition and throwing of liquid or dry colour or even plain white powder continue to be the main items of celebrations" (*ibid.*: 8-9). The other festivals celebrated by Hindus are the birthday of Ram (Ramanavami), Krishna's birthday (Janmashthami), the wedding night of Shiva (Shiva-ratri) and Katik Nahan (ceremonial bathing) in the month of October-November. The most popular Puja in Trinidad is that of Satyanarayan.

Overwhelming majority of the present generation of Hindus in Trinidad are the followers of Sanatan Dharma. The *Sanatan Dharam Maha Sabha* had played a significant role in the revival of Hindu culture in Trinidad. Till 1952 there were two organizations of the Sanatanists—the Sanatan Dharam Association and the Sanatan Dharam Board of Control. But due to efforts of some prominent leaders, the two organizations merged into one and became *Sanatan Dharam Maha Sabha*. The activities of the Sanatan Dharam Mahasabha created a sense of unity among Indians by celebrating Hindu festivals and India's Independence Day. Such activities also has important political implications, as it is through the Maha Sabha that recruitment of leadership takes place.

The Sanatan Dharma Maha Sabha of Trinidad is mainly dominated by those Brahmans who are literate only in Hindi or Sanskrit as the western educated Brahman youth have moved to other occupations. "This body sets the standards for the practice of Hinduism in Trinidad and has successfully driven opposition groups such as the Arya Samaj out of existence. It even claims the right to pass on the admission to Trinidad of all itinerant swamis and gurus from India. The Maha Sabha has acquired...sole authority over the social and educational concerns of Hindus in Trinidad. It has sponsored the creation of a network of schools, and has worked for the passage of laws—permitting cremation, Hindu marriage, etc.—desired by the Hindu community" (Klass, 1991: 157). Though the body invites the non-Brahmans to various functions, the latter are not part of the decision-making process. Since the body functions in an autocratic way by controlling the temples and even denying the services of Hindu pundit to perform a marriage or to conduct prayers, many educated and wealthy non-Brahman Hindus find solace in The Satya Sai Baba movement.

The Satya Sai Baba movement provided an alternative to those Hindus in Trinidad who were alienated from traditional Hinduism and yet tied to it. The movement does not interfere with the traditional Hinduism as devotees can still invite a pandit to perform marriages and other religious ceremonies. The most salient feature of Sai Baba movement is that it does not distinguish on the basis of caste and religion. Any person irrespective of caste "...may play the instruments, join in the singing of bhajans, perform arati, and...lead the singing: there is nothing in the service that either requires or rejects the participation of the Brahman pandit" (*ibid.*: 160). Moreover, the caste inequality is totally obliterated by the Sai Baba movement. Any person having faith in Sai Baba can join the movement. There were fifteen formal places in Trinidad in 1985 where devotees met regularly for prayers.

Besides these central organizations there are some other organizations which also organize activities of Hindu Youths. The activities of these organizations have created gaps between young Hindus and the central Hindu organizations (Vertovec,

1994). Such organizations function not only in urban areas but also in rural Trinidad where Indians are settled. Such groups call themselves as *mandals* and organize functions such as annual *yagnas* and more frequent Ramayan *satsangs*. Religious activities are also organized some time by small group of people who may join hands to celebrate various festivals such as Diwali and Holi. Hindu families also perform various kinds of pujas in their homes in which close friends and relatives are invited. All these reveals that Indians in Trinidad have not forgotten their traditional religious festivals and celebrate in their own ways.

Three other religious sects besides Sanatan Dharam Sabha and Satya Sai Movement among Hindus in Trinidad are the Kabir Panth and Seunarianies, and the Arya Samaj. First two had rejected caste hierarchy and also the rituals. They performed their ceremonies without the help of a Pandit. The majority of the followers of these sects belonged to low caste. On the other hand, Arya Samaj which also rejected many of the symbols of Sanatan Dharam has followers among High caste Hindus. They accepted many western ideas. Arya Samaj came to Trinidad when Arya Samaj missionaries from India who were visiting British Guiana also visited Trinidad. Arya Samaj is the only Hindu sect which the Hindu immigrants to Trinidad did not bring with them. The influence of Arya Samaj is confined to central Trinidad and the number of its followers is not very large (Malik, 1971: 32).

After the recession in economy in eighties there was decline in religious activities as people could not afford. As individuals were unable to sponsor such events, groups were formed which took donations from people and held yagnas and organized other functions such as celebration of *Diwali* and *Holi*, also called *Phagwa*. The family rituals such as *pujas* and *satsangs* are still performed but with much less frills.

Every body including Hindus in Trinidad celebrate Christmas, though a festival of Christians, "because Christmas Day is a day of public celebration, observed by people of all classes and castes, and because that celebration has something to do with its nature as a religious day" (Klass, 1961: 163). The celebrations continue until New Year's Day. People enjoy drinking, eating, and partying during this period. Hindus in Trinidad believe that the "Virgin of Siaparia" near the Roman Catholic Church in Siaparia in Southern Trinidad is an incarnation of Hindu deity. They call it "Sopari-me". Many Hindus take their baby to this place on the first Good Friday for first hair cut (*ibid.*). This shows that Hindus have adopted some aspects of Christian culture and gave them a Hindu colour, thus integrating them into their sandwich culture.

The above description reveals that Indians had maintained their traditional culture and values even after more than one hundred and fifty years of diasporic existence, and they have successfully transmitted them to their children. The great grandchildren of the original immigrants have adopted them though in a slightly modified form. Earlier they were celebrating all the cultural and religious functions at the family level but after the oil boom of the mid-1970s these celebrations are held with great gusto. The celebrations were restored to modest form after the slump in economy in eighties.

Relations with Negroes

Different cultural forms and social institutions of Indians in Trinidad became anamalgam of many North Indian patterns. It reinforced a sub-group identity among them which insulated them from other groups, particularly the Negroes. Their interactions with Negroes remained very limited. Indians consider their culture superior to Creole culture. They resisted "Creolization of Indians". Indians believe that "...Creolization and Westernization are two separate processes; Westernization does not mean the acceptance of the Creole moral values or way of living" (Malik, 1971: 21).

The conflict between Indians and Negroes intensified after independence in 1962 with the formation of two political parties, i.e. People's National Movement (P.N.M.) of Negroes and Democratic Labour Party (D.L.P.) of Indians. The main source of conflict was the question of national identity, i.e. "to which ethnic group does the nation belong and with which culture does it tend to identify" (Gosine, 1993: 162). The party in power perpetuated the interest of its own ethnic group and the other group was not allowed to express freely. The main resentment of Indians against the P.N.M. was that when in power the Negroes controlled the political process and endorsed the policies which favoured them, suppressing, at the same time the culture of Indians. Negroes refuted the allegations and argued that each culture was equally represented in the portrayal of national identity. Indians were charged for not assimilating into the Trinidadian way of life. Indians have accused Negroes for using the power to create a Black bias in public life and not granting cultural freedom to them. Indians also complained that in matters of religion, art and music priority was given to Christianity whereas the representations of the Hindus and Muslims were ignored. The preference to Negroes in the public sector is again attributed to partial behaviour of the government. All these factors taken together affected the social relations between the Indians and the Negroes in Trinidad.

There were three more issues which had bearing on the relations between Indians and Negroes (Jayaram, 2006). One issue was related to Arrival Day Holiday. Indians demanded that May 30—the day when in 1845 Indian immigrants reached Trinidad. The demand gained momentum in 1970 when People's National Movement (P.N.M.), the party led by Africans, came to power and was supported by many Indo-Trinidadian associations and leaders. The issue was also raised in Trinidadian Parliament and a Committee was formed to look into the issue, as some members of Parliament wanted the rationalization of the system of public holidays. The Committee recommended that 30 May should be designated as Arrival Day holiday and not as Indian Arrival Day. When the motion was put to vote in the Parliament it was passed by 18-0 as the opposition boycotted the House. As a result 30 May 1995 was declared holiday but Indians did not accept the decision as they wanted that it shoud be designated as Indian Arrival Day. To counter the move various organizations of Hindus argued that word *Emancipation* should be deleted from African Emancipation Day but this was rejected by the leaders of Afro-Trinidadian group. In 1995, when coalition government of the United National Congress (representing Indo-Trinidadian) and National Alliance for

Reconstruction (party led by a Tobagonian of African origin) came to power they included Indian to the Indian Arrival Day.

The second issue was related to the 'Trinity Cross' a highest civilian award established in August 1969 by Queen Elizabeth II of England to honour the Trinidadians for their services to the society. The names of some Hindu and Muslim leaders were also recommended for the honour but questions were raised on the word Trinity as well on Cross. As both the words had religious tone the leaders of other communities especially the Hindus and the Muslims did not accept. Since it required constitutional amendment and the coalition government did not had requisite majority the matter was dropped.

Another case related to a Muslim girl of Indian origin who was admitted in a Christian school. Objections were raised by the Principal of the school when she attended the school in her Muslim garb known as *hijab*. When the case was referred to the court, the Judge gave his decision in favour of the girl. But again questions were raised by many organizations running school that if children of all the communities attend schools in their own dress then it would be difficult to maintain discipline.

All these three cases are of different nature but reflect diversity of demands of Indo-Trinidadian diasporic community versus Afro-erinidadians. Interestingly, all these questions were raised in the year of the essquicentenary of the arrival of the Indians in Trinidad (Jayaram, 2006). In such circumstances integration and assimilation of Indians with other groups in Trinidad is a remote possibility but in order to survive some adjustments are needed.

III

The analysis of cultural adaptation of Indians in Trinidad is mainly related to indentured labour and all the studies reveal that not much change has taken place among these people. The traditions which were followed by their forefathers when they migrated to Trinidad had been transferred to the present generation and they have adapted them to suit local conditions. In the process, they have also adopted many aspects of Creole culture and English way of life. This assimilation of traits has however not erased their Indian identity. But the Indian culture of the Trinidadian Indians is the product of sandwiching between their parent culture and the culture of the place of their settlement, namely Trinidad.

Summary of apertures and insulatory mechanisms operating in Trinidad have been presented below:

Aperture Opening

(i) Intermarriage or breakdown of endogamy

Contextual conditions did not allow Indians to practice endogamy. As the number of female migrants was much less, high caste Hindus were taking low caste females as partners. Marriages between Hindus and those Hindus who converted to Christianity are accepted as the culture of such union will have more Indian traits. Marriages are also taking place between Hindus and Muslims from India for the same reason. Marriages between Indians and Negroes are not approved in majority of the cases. This means that Indians are not ready to marry the people of host society but are ready to marry other Indians irrespective of their religion.

(ii) Adoption of names of the host society

In the beginning of migration some people made attempt to anglicize their names but later on reverted to their original names. Under the influence of living in a different environment the spelling and pronunciations of the names of Indians have undergone change. Some influence of host society is visible. The names of the Indians show that they still identify themselves with the region from where they migrated which indicates that they still connect themselves with the parent culture.

(iii) Adoption of the language

Younger generation of Indians generally speak standard English or creole English but the older generation prefer to use their own dialect. A common language called Hindustani was used to communicate with each other. Hindi could not become the language of the masses despite all the infrastructure available.

(iv) Religious conversion

Few cases of religious conversion are there but these people still read Hindu religious books. Majority have not changed their religion.

(v) Adoption of food habits and developing taste for host cuisine

By and large Indians have maintained their food habits. There is resemblance in Trinidad curry and the Indian curry. Some Indian dishes have made inroads in Trinidad cuisine but majority of Indians prefer to take Indian food.

Insulatory Mechanisms

(i) Retention of mother tongue

Younger generation have adopted English as their mother tongue. But the older generation use their mother tongue.

(ii) Concentration in residential pattern

There are few pockets in Trinidad where there is concentration of Indians which insulates them from members of the host society. Their interaction with the members of the host society is limited.

(iii) Separate educational facilities

Before 1940 Indians were not sending their children to schools run by Christians. But after the *Sanatan Dharam Maha Sabha* opened schools and also hired Indian teachers, Indians started sending their children to these schools. Arrangements are also made to teach Hindi to children.

(iv) Endogamy

Instead of endogamy, hypergamous marriages became the accepted practice. Another feature is that to maintain the traits of Indian culture the marriages between Hindus and Muslims are also taking place. This kind of sandwich culture will be the mix of Hindu and Muslim traits. Marriages are also taking place between Hindus and those Hindus who became Christians.

(v) Concentration in certain occupations

As indentured labour they were working in sugar plantations. But after the lapse of their contract they were allowed to shift to other occupations. Some of them including Brahmans adopted their traditional occupation but majority did not continue in traditional occupations.

(vi) Voluntary organizations

Hindus have formed religious organizations. Sanatan Dharam Maha Sabha is the main organization. Few Indians who not did like the dominance of Brahmans became a part of Satya Sai Baba Movement. There were some other organizations called *mandals* who organized religious functions. Followers of Kabir Panth and Arya Samaj have formed their own organizations. Through these organizations Indians keep the parent culture alive.

(vii) Parental religion

Except few Hindus who converted to Christianity, majority of Indians did not change their religion.

(viii) Cultural diacriticals

There is not much difference in the dressing pattern of males except Pandits who are engaged in religious activities. They have retained their traditional dress including *tilak* in forehead. Older women still wear sarees but the younger generation females have started wearing jeans and skirt. On special occasions men wear their traditional dress of dhoti and kurta.

(ix) Continuation of food habits and taboos

Majority of Indians are continuing their old food habits except the younger generation people who have developed liking for non-vegetarian Trinidad food which has some resemblance with Indian food.

(x) Contact with parent culture

The contextual and situational conditions of those who migrated as indentured labour did not permit them to maintain contact with the people back home. But later on after Trinidad became an independent country Indians were exposed to their parent culture through films and occasional visits by various cultural groups.

IV

Summing Up

Even after one hundred fifty years majority of the traits of parent culture can still be found. They have not opened apertures with the people of host society but have developed sandwich culture which is a mixture of traits of Indian culture. This has been possible as there are inter-caste and inter religious marriages among Indians. Cultural persistence and renaissance among Indians in Trinidad became possible due to inner vitality of the Indian culture which had survived in adverse conditions. Its resilience power helped it to recuperate even when the conditions were not favourable. Moreover no serious attempt was ever made either by the host society as well the migrants from India to create apertures. Negative feeling and cultural incompatibility are other contributory factors which did not allow Indians to create apertures. On the contrary Indians are insulated from the host society from the beginning and this amalgamation of Indians proved beneficial in revival of their parent culture.

The cultural, and contextual conditions of Indians in Trinidad did not allow them to have much interaction with the Negroes as well as the White people. Language was the main barrier as an interpreter was required even at work. The British never directly interacted with Indians and it was only through middle man that they were communicating with them. Chances of opening apertures were almost non-existent but on the other hand insulatory mechanism were more in operation. Even when their contract as indentured labour was over, no apertures were created and situation did not change. Economically also they were at the lower rung of the scale. Neither Indians nor Whites and Negroes made any attempt to create apertures while in Trinidad. Certain cultural traits of the East Indians in Trinidad, did not allow them to develop personal contact with other ethnic groups. The process of revival of Indian culture began once they were free from indentured contract and the process enhanced after India became independent in 1947. This encouraged them to open their own schools, and also built mosques and temples and made arrangements to teach Hindi and Urdu to their children. Though only small percentage of Indians were able to understand the dialogues of Hindi movies, even then they wanted to watch them, because they found it closer to their lives and conform to their basic values. Indian music was a regular features in wedding and other festivals. Thus, it can be inferred that they did not made any attempt to adapt the cultural traits of the host society and maintained their own identity. Malik (1971) agrees with Braithwaite (1954) that despite the strong cultural ethnic cleavages and feeling of racial exclusiveness, the tolerance level has been appreciated. In fact, both have placed Trinidad society at Gordon's tolerance level of cultural pluralism. According to M.M. Gordon, "At the tolerance level of group relations ethnic groups would maintain such a high degree of social isolation from each other that virtually all primary contacts would be within the ethnic group and most secondary contacts would be either correspondingly confined or it across ethnic lines, completely accommodating, various ethnic groups would be encouraged to have a tolerant attitude towards one another" (Gordon, M.M., 1959: 829, quoted from Malik, 1971: 24).

Indians though belonged to different castes and ethnic groups revived number of their key institutions which they brought with them, which helped them to reproduce and maintain the basic elements of their native culture. This was considered a necessity if they wanted to maintain their distinct identity as "East Indians in their value orientation, life goals, beliefs and institutional structures differ from other ethnic groups with respect to marriage, family, kinship, way of life, religious ceremonies, festivals, dance and music they have distinctive traditions and customs" (Malik, 1971: 7). Brahmans who came as indentured labour, though their number was small, played pivotal role in revising Indian traditions and customs which were of immense help to maintain their identity as Indians. Even those well to do Indians in urban areas of Trinidad who had accepted some aspects of Western culture did not accept the Creole cultural values of Negroes.

In Trinidad East Indians and Negroes tolerated each other without having any social interaction and also did not use violence against each other. Therefore, we can safely say that East Indians remained Indian despite being in Trinidad for many years. They were at the minimum level of sandwich culture.

CHAPTER-3

Hindus and Sikhs in the United States of America

Indians are the third largest group, besides Chinese and Filipinos, among the Asians residing in the United States of America. Between 1990 and 2000, the growth of Indians in USA was around 106 per cent. The United States Immigration and Naturalization Service Report for the year 2001 specified that Indians were the second highest migrants between October 1, 2000 and September 6, 2001. Of the total 1,064,318 permanent migrants during that period, 70,290 were from India. In 1965, only 4,000 persons were recorded under the Alien Address Programme; the number increased to 109,000 by 1977 of whom 88 per cent were permanent residents, and another 1,300 took American citizenship. Number of Indian immigrants in America during 1965-77 registered an increase of 3,000 per cent (Leonard-Spark and Saran, 1980). By 1980, the number of Indians residing in the United States increased to 387,223 and in 1990 it reached 815,447 (Rangaswamy, 2000). According to rough estimates, now the number of Indians in the USA must be around two million.

People from almost all the states of India have migrated to the United States of America. But the Punjabis and Gujaratis have outnumbered others. Among Punjabis it is the Sikh community which have migrated in large numbers. The number of Gujaratis is highest among Hindus. In this study we are concentrating on the adaptation pattern of Punjabis mainly Sikhs and Hindus in USA (number of Sikhs is about 500,000 taken from Internet, September 2008 and among Hindus the number of Gujaratis is 400,000 as reported by Gopa Kumar, 2003). Though Sikhs are living in almost all parts of USA, yet their main concentration is in Yuba City, California. Out of over 500,000 Sikhs in USA around 100,000 constituting 20 per cent, are living in California. The other areas where Sikhs are spread out include Stockton and Baker Field, CA, Atlanta, GA, The Richman Hill neighbourhood of Queens, New York City, NY, Chicago, IL, Seattle, WA, Detroit, MI and Oregon. The main concentration of Hindus is in New York, Illinois, California, Texas, North Carolina, New Jersey and Connecticut.

History and Pattern of Migration

The first significant immigration of Indians to the United States of America occurred in 1901 when about seven thousand Sikhs of Malwa and Doaba region of Punjab migrated to Canada to work on the Canadian Pacific Railways. The drought and famine conditions, as also changes in the land tenure system in Punjab, forced some of them to migrate to the United States of America to work in the lumber mills of Bellingham and Everett (Washington). Some of them decided to move to California. Before that some Indian merchants occasionally visited New York and San Francisco. In 1907, there was a revolt against Indian migrants who were working in the lumber mills of the United States Pacific North-West because local labourers perceived these Indians as threat to them as they were working on less wages compared to local people. Newspapers also supported the locals as they thought it was invasion by Hindus and Sikhs on the American Labour market.

Though the number of Indians migrants, most of whom were Sikhs, was not more than 6,000 between 1904 and 1923, their distinctive turbans, beards, language, and dress made them noticeable. The United States Government also issued exclusion order from United States against Asians including Indians. In 1904, majority of the Indian immigrants were Sikhs, though there were few Hindus and Muslims also. During summer months they worked on the farms in the Sacrament, San Joaquin and Imperial valley and shifted to Yuba city, Stockton and El Centro California in winter.

There were a few educated Indians who came for higher education. There were some political refugees who migrated to escape British repression. These early migrants had to face many hurdles including discriminatory laws which forced some of these people to leave. In 1946, the Luce-Celler Bill was passed which gave Asian Indians the right to become American citizens, own property, and bring relatives to America. This also enabled the families to migrate to America and reunite with their husbands.

Some of the Indian migrants played a significant role in the freedom struggle of India. A Bengali student, Mr. Tarak Nath Das, who was studying at the University of Washington joined hands with an Irish-American publisher and started publishing the *Free Hindustan* in 1908, which was suppressed after three years due to British intervention. *Ghadr Party* was also formed in San Francisco under the leadership of Lala Har Dayal who was also the editor of the weekly newspaper *Ghadr*. This weekly newspaper was published in various Indian languages such as Gurmukhi, Urdu, Hindi, Bengali and Marathi. This revolutionary movement of Indians in America continued till 1917, when the leaders were arrested in California. Of the 29 East Indians charged, 14 were convicted. Though the paper continued, after the trial, under the name of *Hindustan Ghadr*, it had lost its effectiveness. The activities of the Ghadr party ended in 1947, after India gained independence.

Another leader who kept the Indian freedom movement alive in America was Lala Lajpat Rai who came to the United States in 1914. A moderate group of Indians formed the Home Rule League on the East coast of the United States in 1910. Lala Lajpat Rai became the leader of this group in 1917 and assumed the editorship of the periodical *Young India*. This Home Rule League had also the support of some Americans. Jayaprakash Narayan was also a student at the University of Wisconsin. All these people took keen interest in the affairs of India and tried to influence American public opinion.

American immigration Act of 1965, changed the nature of immigrant population from unskilled, uneducated and self-employed to professionally oriented and technically trained personnel. The new Act encouraged the immigrants not only from India but from other Asian countries also. The new Act also helped the migration of relatives of those already settled in America.

The major influx of migration of Indians in USA began after 1965 when significant changes were made in the immigration law. Prior to 1965, besides Jat Sikhs, it was the student community who predominantly migrated to the United States to pursue higher studies. There were very few who migrated as permanent residents. The American immigration law of 1965 increased the quota to 20,000 immigrants including from India for those who wanted to take permanent resident status in any given year. In 1965, only 582 Indians were granted permanent resident status but the number increased to 2,458 in 1966, showing an increase of 4.2 per cent and by 1977, the number reached to 18,613 (c.f. Leonard-Spark and Saran, 1980: 144). The quota of 20,000, has many preferential categories favouring professional and technical persons and also the relatives and dependants of those who either lived as resident aliens or became U.S. citizen.

The history of Indian immigration to the United States of America has been divided into following five periods (La Brack, 1983):

1. The first period includes Sikh migrants who came to the West Coast of the USA from Canada between 1904-23. About 10,000 were admitted but at any time there number did not exceed more than 6,000.
2. The second period includes illegal migrants who came from Mexico between 1923 to early 1930. Their number was around 3,000.
3. The period between 1930 to 46 can be called as lull period when the migration was negligible.
4. The period between 1946 to 64 has been called as Quota period of restricted immigration.
5. Open migration began in 1965 with the changes in the immigration policy. Those who came after 1965 can further be classified in three categories. This includes:

   (a) Those who were sponsored by the early settlers in USA mainly Sikhs in California. As the new immigration law gave highest priority to the reunification of families, about two-third of the visas were granted to relatives of American citizens and permanent residents. The proportion of Punjabis sponsored by the relatives of California was very high (Gibson, 1988). Most of them came from rural areas of Punjab and did not possess any technical skill.

(b) The second category includes all those who migrated as professionals and technical persons.

(c) Another group of Indians who came to USA were those who migrated from East Africa due to political upheavals especially in Kenya and Uganda in 1970s. Most of them were businessmen who migrated along with their families including parents and grandparents. They mainly settled in urban centres.

Since the cultural, contextual and situational conditions of these migrants varied significantly from the earlier migrants, the adaptation process of these new migrants differed substantially from the earlier settlers. The overwhelming majority of Sikhs who came to California for settlement were farmers and not well educated and belonged to Jat caste. Migrants who were sponsored by the early settlers came from rural Punjab and belonged to same region of Doab. They came with the intention to settle permanently. Majority of them brought their families. They came as they were promised all help including financial from the early settlers. Very few could speak English and had no technical training except farming. They came as they believed that America is a land of opportunities and it would be good for them as well as for their children. Thus, the cultural conditions of new migrants were similar to the earlier settlers but the contextual and situational conditions differed significantly. They not only belonged to same region but also shared religious and caste affiliation.

The migrants who came to USA after the changes in immigration law in 1965, included those who came as students but later on changed to permanent resident status. There were few who came to settle permanently. Among those who came on student visa, some came with their spouses and children, a few brought their spouses and children after a stay of one or two years. Some of those who were unmarried went back to India to get married and returned with their spouses. There were a few others who married Indians in America. There are very few cases, where Indian students have married either an American or some body other than American or Indian. Among those who came on permanent immigrant visa, some came with their families, or brought their families after a stay of one year.

Indians who migrated to the United States after 1965, had an edge over earlier migrants and the migrants sponsored by them. Majority of these new migrants were professionals and possessed specialized skills which were in great demand in USA at that time. They were also fluent in English as they were well educated. They came from almost all the States of India. In a survey conducted in the New York Metropolitan Area in 1977-78 by Leonard-Spark and Saran it was found that about one-third of the immigrants were from the State of Gujarat and about 20 per cent from Hindi speaking regions including Delhi. However, the pattern of emigration from India changed after 1965, when the new immigration law was enacted. During 1966-68, Indian immigrants from Gujarat accounted for 44 per cent but this ratio came down to 28 after 1974. The decline was also noticed among immigrants from Maharashtra and Bihar, but the States of Kerala, Andhra Pradesh, and Punjab recorded phenomenal growth during the same period. The pattern of migration after 1965 thus shifted "(F)rom the North toward the Middle and South of India, that is away from the areas that were historically under the greatest English colonial influence toward those with different language and cultural patterns and less direct influence by the British Raj. The shifts also suggest that within the Indian community here there is increasingly greater diversity in the ethnic-regional backgrounds of the Indians who comprise it" (Leonard-Spark and Saran, 1980: 143).

Settlement Pattern

Punjabi Jat Sikhs who migrated from Vancouver in Canada settled in different parts of California but their main concentration was in the Imperial, Sacromento, and San Joaquin valley areas. They were uneducated farmers whose age varied between forty and fifty years. All of them hailed from the Doaba region of Eastern Punjab and belonged to the same religion and caste. Thus, they shared common values and attitudes. Some of these Sikhs were *Amritdharis* (baptized members of the Khalsa), who pledged to maintain the traditional Sikh values and customs as well as five K's.[10] There were others known as *Sahajdharis* who were not bound to keep the outward symbols of their faith. They cut their hair short and also shaved their beard.

Prejudice and discrimination against the immigrant groups by the members of the host society is imminent, especially if the immigrant group is economically doing better than the members of the host society. The Sikhs of California in the initial stages also found themselves in the same situation, but did not react simply because this was the price to be paid for economically better off compared to their position in India. Direct interaction between Punjabi Jat Sikhs and the Valley Side Americans was very limited as most of the old timer Punjabis lived outside town on their large ranches. Since most of the Jat Sikhs were working in farms they did not come in direct contact with Valley Side Americans. The Valleysiders came in contact with Punjabis either in shops or in banks. Most of the Valleysiders did not regard Sikhs as part of them as they were different and speak different language. The attitude of Valleysiders towards Punjabis became more negative with the increase in their number. The attitude of Punjabis towards Valley Side Americans was mixed. Though the Punjabis had bad experience, yet they described those acts as isolated incidents. Most of them tried to play down the negative and prejudiced behaviour of the Valleysiders. They also held teenagers responsible rather than adults for biased behaviour. Punjabis did not harbour negative attitude towards Americans, as a group. Punjabis did not like the actions of certain individuals, but on the whole showed respect for the members of the majority group. Some Punjabis also appreciated the co-operation and help they got from their Valleyside neighbours. On the whole, Punjabis appreciated and liked the fairness and openness of the American system. The negative attitude and behaviour of some members of the majority group did not dampen their spirit. As compared to the conditions of their friends and relatives in other countries especially in England and Canada, they considered themselves better-off in America. To avoid any confrontation with the members of the majority of group, Punjabis preferred to keep themselves away from them. They were happy as long as economically they were doing better than the majority group.

Regarding the settlement pattern of Indians in USA who migrated after 1965 Rangaswamy writes that "Indians seemed to prefer to live close to work or in neighbourhoods where property values held up rather than to cluster together in a single area. The general tendency was toward dispersal in the white suburbs. Sometime the development of a strong commercial complex in a specific area may have encouraged residential concentration in the same area, as in the case of Devon Avenue in Chicago, but the more affluent they became, the more Indians tended to get away from such concentrations" (Rangaswamy, 2000: 54). By and large Indians move safely in USA except in some area where they are living amongst lower income groups who feel threatened by the prosperity of the newcomers as happened to Punjabis in California. It happened in Jersey city when some working class White youth calling themselves "dotbusters" (dot refers to the bindi used by Indian women on their forehead) assaulted and even killed Indians on the street. This had its repercussions on the settlement pattern of Indians in USA.

Vocational Activities

Early migrants from India were working as farm labourers. Since family members were not allowed to migrate they had no family life. In fact, their employment as well as their living arrangements were temporary. As majority of them hailed from the same region they joined hands to from 'labour gangs' (La Brack, 1983). In the process they also revived their kinship relationship based on sub-caste, lineage and village affiliation. Besides sharing the residence they also shared the expenses and hired a cook to prepare Punjabi meals. Working as farm labourers they gained experience and knowledge about land, working conditions, irrigation methods, machinery, as well as about transportation and processing systems which came handy once they became landowners. As the Alien Land Laws of 1913 and 1922 prevented them to own the land they "...put the title in an American citizen's name, which could be an American-born or naturalized wife, wife's relative, or even a trusted American friend. Another method was used in the 1930s and 1940s to place the title in the names of American-born children from marriages which took place between Sikhs and European or Mexican women" (*ibid.*: 219). The ownership of land by Sikhs was not appreciated by the locals and there were agitations in many parts, but the Sikhs managed to survive with the help and support of well-wishers and friends. Gradually, they purchased more land and became prosperous.

The Sikhs who were sponsored by the early settlers also settled in California along with their relatives and friends who were already there. They also took to farming in America the occupation they were pursuing before migration, as this was the only option available to them. They were encouraged and helped by their well-wishers. They enjoyed the rural atmosphere and as it was similar to Punjab. Those who were working as farm labourers were earning much more in comparison to their income in India. Despite living in USA for many years there was not much change in their way of life. Financially, they were better off in USA as compared to India. Life in USA was comfortable in comparison to Punjab due to availability of all sorts of food including ready made clothes, washing machines, and televisions, air-conditioned houses (Gibson, 1988). The Punjabi immigrants were also impressed by "the openness and fairness of American institutions and the laws that safeguard individual rights" (*ibid.*: 51). They appreciated the fact that in USA even a child of a small farmer can achieve high status which is not possible in India as the system in India is "more personalistic, more tied to family connections, influence and wealth" (*ibid.*: 51).

The attitude of Jat Sikhs towards their womenfolk changed noticeably after living in America. In India, Jat women never worked in the field, but after living in America for many years they changed their lifestyle and started working outside home for money. It was in the 1970s that the first Jat woman broke the tradition. She became the object of teasing in the beginning, but gradually her new role was accepted by others. Now Jat women contribute substantially to the family income. They also found that women, who are unable to find steady work, are eligible to get unemployment compensation during the months they are laid off. The attitude of Punjabis towards their daughters also changed. They allow their daughters to have sufficient education which enables them to obtain a 'clean' and secure job in banks, schools, and offices. Thus, the Punjabi Jat Sikhs have adapted themselves to the new conditions to further their economic interests.

There was another group of Indians who migrated under the preferential categories of professionals and technical persons and also the relatives of dependants of those who either lived as resident aliens or took US citizenship. It included people of both the sexes. All of them were highly educated and technically skilled professionals who made their mark in a relatively short period of time. They were, in fact, welcomed in the United States because of their professional skills or potential technical contributions. They migrated to settle permanently but at the same time maintained their relations with the people back home. Some of those who migrated as professionals and technical persons later on shifted to other types of occupations that were financially more remunerative. With the increase in Indian population some enterprising entrepreneurs especially Gujaratis started business of supplying Indian groceries and other items to Indians. Some opened restaurants and retail stores and few started insurance and travel agencies. One consequence of all these developments was that Indian community not only became stable but also self-sufficient. There were some Gujaratis who besides working as professionals were also running business with the help of wife, children and other family members. Few left the job to concentrate full time in business. Indians with professional degrees also faced the problem when their degrees were not recognised and they were required to get an American degree. As a consequence some abandoned their professional career and stared business though they were granted visa on the basis of their professional qualification but it did not guarantee them a job according to their qualification (Fisher, 1980). According to U.S. Government records in 1974 "...about 46,000 Indian immigrants were employed. Of these, approximately 16,000 were employed as engineers, 4,000 as scientists, and 7,000 as physicians or surgeons (Fisher, 1980: 20). Despite all this, many Indians were not able to find work commensurate with their qualifications. Some of them repeated the course but even then they could not get the suitable job as a result many remained unemployed and survived on unemployment allowance.

By 1990 the "...Indian population was a multi-layered community, with affluent professionals and business persons at the top and an increasing number of middle- and working-class immigrants in lower strata" (Khandelwal, 2002: 6). In fact, "most post-1965 immigrants to the United States fitted broadly into a white collar, middle-class continuum. But a growing number of those arriving in the 1980s and 1990s did not fare as well, and a sizable number among them were even clearly downwardly mobile" (*ibid.*: 6). According to 1990 Census of USA 30 per cent of Indian workers were in professional occupations and majority of them were in health profession. Some of them were working as engineers and scientists. Indians are also working as private practitioners in various professions such as medicine, law, engineering, accounting and business. Few Indians, mainly Punjabis are working as taxi drivers and owners in large metropolitan centres. Majority of Gujaratis are in hotel business and running other small business (Gopa Kumar, 2003).

The shifts in the American economy in the 1980 made things difficult for immigrants especially for those who came after 1975. The fiscal crisis in 1975 and stock market crash in 1987 affected the employment conditions. As a consequence "...number of immigrants moved into the underground economy of cash transactions, tax avoidance, and sub-minimum wages. Global economic change since the late 1980s, particularly the upsurge of Asian economies...have created shifts in Asian immigration flows to the United States" (Khandelwal, 2002: 95). As a result some of the Indian professional in the USA began to relocate to India. Some of the immigrants who came after 1980 faced difficulty in securing a job and had tough time to survive. Some of the Indian businessmen employed new immigrants from India but the conflict between employer and employee created more tension than ethnic solidarity.

Family and Marriage

As the early settlers were not allowed to bring brides from India some of them decided to remain single whereas there were others who married non-Indian women. Sikhs who were engaged in farming married Mexican women and those in teaching profession and students married American-born or foreign-born women of European descent. "By 1930s a pattern of intermarriage was established between rural Sikh men and Spanish-speaking women, facilitated by...compatible cultural views of food, male-female roles and family life" (La Brack, 1983: 222). By marrying Mexican and other European American women the social life of the Sikhs became a mix of Punjabi, Spanish and Euro-American traits. The social life of the Sikhs changed. They became members of Mexican American society and participated in their family functions. The names of the children born to such union were given mixed names such as Jesus Singh and Esmeralda. There was a steady decline in Punjabi customs. Even visits to Gurdwara was restricted to three or four times a year mainly on certain occasions such as Guru Nanak's birthday. Children were raised as Catholics the religious faith of their wives and they could not learn any thing about Sikh religion. They did not learn Punjabi language and did not know the social system of their father. The relatives of wife became frequent visitors and in few cases lived in the same house. As a consequence the social foundation of Sikhs based on religion, caste and joint family became superfluous (La Brack, 1983).

Under the Immigration Act of 1946, Indians became legalized immigrants in USA which allowed them to become naturalized citizens. This also gave married men choice to reunite with their wives and children in India and for bachelors to select brides from India and also to sponsor other relatives. But this Act allowed only a quota of 100 Indians per year. However, the change in immigration policy in 1965 allowed more migrants from Punjab. The new migrants who settled in California received all kind of support from the early settlers. Besides providing accommodation also supported them financially. The new migrants who were sponsored by the early settlers influenced the old timers and the Sikhs of California began to revive their culture and customs. The Sikhs who had married Mexican women began divorcing them in favour of Jat Sikh brides. The period between 1947 and 1967 can be called as the revival period when " ...Questions of Sikh identity became increasingly associated with strict, orthodox Punjabi behavioural norms and Khalsa religious practices" (La Brack, 1983: 227). This brought significance changes in the life of Sikhs in California. Joint family system was restored and with that family functions were held regularly and members cooperated with each other. Endogamous marriages became the norm and number of spouses imported from India increased substantially. Sikhs started growing beard and use of turban became more common. Women also started using traditional dress of *salwar kameez* and *saree* (La Brack, 1983).

Indians who came after 1965, irrespective of the fact whether came on student visa or as permanent immigrant, preferred to select an Indian spouse. Their first preference was to select a spouse from India, failing that they preferred to marry an Indian already living in America. Those who came to India for marriage, married a person selected by their family members who belonged to the same religion and caste. But those who selected a spouse among Indians in America, in majority of the cases, the region and caste factors were ignored. For instance, a Maharashtrian Brahmin may select a Kayastha spouse from Uttar Pradesh or *vice versa*. There are a few cases of inter-religious marriages where some Indians have married White Americans. In some cases they married even when the relationship was not approved either by one of the parents or both the parents.

In order to maintain continuity and stability in the family the old timers by and large preferred to marry a person of the same caste. Even those who married a person of different caste or region the approval of the family played significant role. But parents are in dilemma when their American born grown up children want to select their own partner. Most of the first generation migrants are against love marriages as they believe that such marriages are short-lived whereas endogamous marriages are more stable. Social compatibility in marriage is considered necessary but it has also been realized by parents that they have to broaden the search. Marriage with a person of different religion is not acceptable to most of the parents. Different yardstick are adopted for sons and daughters. They are more liberal with their sons as compared to daughters as they fear that the reputation of their daughter may affect the marriage prospect of other sisters. Some parents are against the marriage of their son with US reared Indian women as she will be more Americanized. Such parents return to India to choose a bride and they are assisted by the relatives in the process. In some cases a young man who wanted to immigrate to USA via marriage may accept the proposal (Khandelwal, 2002).

One of the major concerns of the first generation immigrants regarding their grown-up sons and daughters is the problem of dating and marriage. Since most of the first generation migrants are not familiar with the concept of dating, they do not approve their children going out on dating. They are more strict with girls. Despite the restrictions, quite a large number of younger generation people do date but do not tell their parents about it though they would prefer to have Indian spouse (Agarwal, 1991 and Sheth, 2001). For most of the Indian immigrants settled in America, dating is related to premarital sexual relations. Parents allow their wards to go out in groups, where children of both the sexes participate. In fact, the parents prefer that their son and daughter bring their friends over to their house for the weekends. By and large, Indians want their children, both boys and girls, to marry the match selected by the parents. That is one of the reasons that most of the parents do not favour their daughters to go to college education. Punjabis while selecting a mate for their ward give preference to region, religion and caste. Earlier Punjabis in USA used to select mate for their ward from

India but now the Punjabi marriages have really become transnational as the marriage partner are selected from all over the globe. As the matrimonial advertisements are available not only in newspapers but also in the internet which makes it easy to negotiate (Gopa Kumar, 2003).

On the grounds of "compatibility" inter-racial marriages are not approved. Parents allow their wards to marry an Indian spouse of their choice, rather than opting for the traditional, arranged marriage. Quite a large number of the second generation people prefer to marry other 'ABCD' (American Born Confused Desi) rather than marrying a person selected by their parents (Agarwal, 1991: 51). Younger generation women are more "averse" to importing a spouse from India as compared to men.

Matrimonial advertisements in ethnic Indian newspaper like *India Abroad* to select a spouse is also frequently used. An analysis of matrimonial advertisements in *India Abroad* in a issue of 1975 was attempted by Maxine Fisher (1980) and it has been repeated by Khandelwal (2002) in a issue of 1988. While comparing the data of two issues, Khandelwal found that in 1975 caste was mentioned in 23 per cent of the cases and religion in 31 per cent advertisements. In 1988 the percentage of caste increased to 33 and that of religion to 45. In 1975, 23 per cent described caste as irrelevant to marriage but in 1988 it declined to 13 per cent. In 1988 advertisements were also given by Indians in Canada, Britain, Hong Kong, the Caribbean, Saudi Arabia and India (Khandelwal, 2002: 155). This indicates that the emphasis on religion and caste while selecting a mate among Indians in USA is gaining momentum and people are going transnational.

Attitude of husbands and wives towards household responsibility has changed after living in USA. Husbands have started sharing household work with wives and wives have taken employment outside the household. However, their attitude towards the institution of marriage has not changed. For them marriage is a life-long commitment unlike their American counterparts. Husband still remains the authority figure. Parents want to transmit their Indian values and traditions to their children but most of the time children are busy either in watching television or indulging in some other activities. Since America is the reference point for children, a gap is created between parents and children. Parents want to protect children from the so-called evils of American society which is not appreciated by the children.

Family in America becomes the main institution of socialization for Indians, as in school they are exposed to American way of life. At home children are taught the traditional pattern of language, diet, dress, religion and other customs, necessary to maintain their identity as Indian. Most of the Indians in America are in constant touch with the family members back in India either through visits or inviting them to visit USA. The visits of elderly persons from India not only provide domestic and household aid, but also serves as a traditional role model for their children in America. Some parents do not allow their children to play with American kids in the neighbourhood to avoid their exposure to the process of Americanization (Nandan and Eames, 1980).

Serious problems are faced problems by the parents when they want to inculcate their own Indian values to their children. Children who are exposed to American way of life in school as well as through media develop an ambivalent attitude towards their parent culture. A rift is created between parents and children. Children very often ask many questions when their parents pressurize them not to follow American values and customs. To solve these problems some parents send their children to India for schooling and there are few cases where parents have decided to return to India. But all parents make serious efforts to expose their children to Indian values, customs and way of life.

Americanization of Indian Names

Many Indians after migrating to USA found that Americans are unable to pronounce their names. In order to make convenient for Americans to pronounce some of the North Indians shorten their names such as Bhupinder became Bob, Jagmohan to Jack, Ravindra to Romi, Priyanka to Priya or

Pinky, Sandhya to Sandy (Fisher, 1980, Sheth, 2001). But as the migrants grow old most of them feel more comfortable with their Indian name as a result "many drop the Americanized version of their names in favour of their given names. For example, Roger reverts to Raj and Michael metamorphosises in to Munjal" (Agarwal, 1991: 37-38).

But the problem becomes serious with the names of South Indians. Naming system in South India is different from other parts of India. Even in South India there are variations from state to state. For instance a Brahmin from Karnataka is given four names. The first name is that of father, the second is name of the village or place of origin, third is the name given to an individual and fourth is the caste name. First two names are abbreviated by their initials. Few South Indians drop their caste name and in that case those who are not familiar with the system assume that third name which is the given name of a person is the surname. The problem becomes acute when a South Indian migrates to America. Since surname is required to get U.S. visa and also for the enrolment of children in schools the given name of the person becomes his surname and all his children use it as surname. "As a result of this phenomenon, a South Indian wife addresses her husband by the name which the family simultaneously uses as its new surname" (Fisher, 1980: 50). Some of the South Indians have divided their given name in two parts and second part becomes new surname. For example, the name Harimohan may become Mr. Hari Mohan and later on Hari may become Harry.

Retention of Cultural Diacriticals

Sikhs, among Indians stand out for turban, beard and steel bangle on their wrist. Even those Sikhs who have cut their hair short keep beard and use steel bangles on their wrist. Because of their physical appearance Sikhs are easily identifiable in any group. In the early stages of their settlement they faced many problems as American could not distinguish between Hindus and Sikhs. Some of them changed their physical appearance but with the arrival of new migrants they reverted back to their original appearance.

Other Indian men generally wear Western dress when they go out and you cannot distinguish them on the basis of dress. But at home all of them might not be using the similar outfit. For instance the traditional dress of most of the South Indian men is white loin cloth called *dhoti*. In USA these South Indian men use traditional dress on two occasions, when they visit temple or when a religious ceremony is performed at home (Fisher, 1980). Men from other states of India do not have any particular dress for various occasions.

Under the influence of American culture, most of the Sikhs, both the conservatives as well non-conservatives, had started cutting their hair and also shaving their beards; this is more so among the younger ones. Often, one can find that in one family eldest son may keep long hair and beard but the younger son may have short hair and remain clean shaved.

The traditional dress of Sikh women is *salwar kameez*, (salwar is tight fitting pyjama like bottom whereas kurta is long sleeve tunic) and in USA also the Sikh women stick to their original dress. The young girls among Sikhs started wearing Western dress like jeans but on formal occasions such as marriage they will wear their traditional dress.

The traditional dress of Indian women except Sikh ladies is *Sari*, though use of salwar kameez by all the ladies, young and old is quote common. Indian ladies continue with this practice even in the United States. Some of them have starting wearing Western dress especially jeans and pants when go to work. But at home they are more comfortable in their traditional dress. On the basis of the traditional dresses of Indian women the region to which they belong can be discerned. South Indian women generally prefer dark colour silk *saris* whereas non South Indian women like to wear pastel colour *saris* of lighter weight material. South Indian women also like brocaded borders of gold on the edge and bottom. Even the style of wearing *sari* can distinguish women from one region to other. (Fisher, 1980 and Khandelwal, 2003). Other diacritical marks used by Indian women is *bindi* on their forehead. For Hindu women use of *bindi* is a sign of marriage, though nowadays some young girls also use it as a part of fashion. In 1980 in New Jersey some young Americans created problems for these women and called themselves as "the Dotbusters". The married females from South India as well as from Gujarat and Maharashtra use *mangal sutra* as a sign of married women (Fisher 1980 and Khandelwal, 2003).

Language

Indians are very particular that their children should learn their mother tongue besides English. Therefore, most Indian families use their regional language at home, but children rarely use it. To expose their kids to regional language, parents take their children to temples and Gurdwaras where most of the ceremonies are held in regional languages. Another way to expose their children to regional language is to show them Indian movies, which may be either in Hindi or in any other regional language. Sometimes, regular classes are also organized by various groups to expose their children to regional language. Though the most of the Indians become bilingual but majority in interpersonal communication use their regional language. The regional languages are also promoted by various associations of Indians. Other way to promote the regional languages is the publication of newspapers in these languages as is done by Punjabis and Gujaratis (Khandelwal, 2002).

The use of native language is declining among children who are born and brought up in the United States. Most of these children may understand the language but are not be able to speak. In fact, those parents who are not fluent in English encourage their children to learn and speak English as was done by the Sikhs in California. The intergenerational communication has also been affected due to language gap between immigrants and USA born children. Parents complain that their children speak English in American accent whereas children feel embarrassed by their parents' English (Khandelwal, 2002).

Food

Food is essential for survival of all living beings, but what has to be eaten, how it has to be cooked and how it has to be eaten is basically determined by culture. It does not only affect the diet and food practices of a society, but food habits and diets also considerably influence the culture of the group. Food habits are determined not only by the availability of the items but also by the preferences that are culturally transmitted. For instance, in America, beef is readily available, but it is religiously tabooed for Hindus and similar taboo is observed by the Muslims for pork. One area in which Indians settled in America are not ready to compromise is their food and eating habits. There might be few exceptions but majority do not change their food habits.

However, a distinct change can be seen amongst Indians in America. Many migrants who were vegetarians shift to non-vegetarian food after settling down in the State. Of course, such a shift is partial. While turning to non-vegetarian food, many Hindus still observe the ban on beef. But change to non-vegetarian food might be for the sake of younger generation born and brought up in the State. Sometime parents eat McDonald's Hamburgers and Kentucky Fried Chicken for the sake of children (Nandan and Eames, 1980). By and large Indians retain their tastes for traditional food of chapatti, spices and vegetables and rice prepared in Indian style. However, there might be some differences between families with children and those without children. Families with children have a more flexible attitude and at least for convenience's sake may cook American style meals as well. However, majority of the Indian immigrants resist any change in their food and eating habits, though they have become more conscious about nutritional value of food. Women avoid items that are fattening and often go on restricted diets. Indians also prefer to invite friends for lunch or dinner at home or some time visit them but avoid eating out in restaurants. Indians do not invite friends only for cocktails like Americans, but also serve food whenever they invite friends at home (Saran, 1985). Indians who are more exposed to American way of life like having an American spouse will have tendency to eat out more often. Indians who have married non-Indians sometime cook their own Indian dishes to satisfy their appetite for Indian food. While cooking food, Indians use flavoured aromatic spices that are commonly used by Indians in India (Nandan and Eames, 1980). In majority of the Indian families food is cooked in traditional pattern, only in few cases American style is preferred (Angelo, 1997). In all the functions organized by various Indian organizations only Indian food is served which may be a mixture of items from various States of India.

Education

The majority of the first generation migrants were uneducated, but they advised their children to attend American schools and also learn American way of life. They wanted their children to take full advantage of educational and economic opportunities available in America. At the same time, they wished that the children should maintain and improve their family's good name. Punjabis asked their children to opt for professional courses or other job-oriented courses at the high school level. They appreciated the American education system which gives professional training to their kids at this level, a facility not available in India. Since educational facilities in America are excellent and medium of instruction is also English, need was not felt to open separate schools for Indians.

Social and Cultural Organization

Early immigrants preferred to form Pan-Indian organizations, but with the increase in number of migrants from various states of India the growth of regional organizations and sectarian religious institutions that cater to specific sub-groups among Indians in America sprang up. The first pan Indian organization was formed in 1960 when professional Indian immigrants joined hands. The main objective was to protect the interest of immigrants ignoring their cultural and religious differences. It was done to retain their separate identity as Indians. Three major Pan-Indian associations namely: The Association of Indians in America (AIA), the Federation of Indians in America (FIA) and the National Federation of Indians in America (NFIA) were formed between 1967 and 1980. They represented Indians in multicultural and multiethnic activities in America. The AIA and NFIA formed local chapters all over the USA. The leaders of these associations were upper-middle-class professionals who were the early immigrants in the country. The AIA succeeded to get "Asian Indian" category in the US census under the "Asian and Pacific Islanders" and Minority status to the immigrants of South Asian Americans for civil rights purposes. Later on it represented the interests of foreign medical graduates within the American Medical Association. It also "conducted voter registration drives and youth projects and ran 'Project India' which through 1991 had channelled more than Fifteen Million dollars worth of funds and equipment to projects and relief works in India" (Khandelwal, 2002: 162).

The Federation of Indian Associations was the principal umbrella group for the growing number of Indian organizations. In 1987-88 it had seventy organizations under it. It mainly concentrated on celebrating certain functions such as Indian Independence Day, Republic Day, Gandhi Jayanti and U.S. Independence Day (Saran and Leonard-Spark, 1980 and Khandelwal, 2002). NFIA had chapters all over the United States and it protected the interests of the middle and upper class immigrant cohorts. In 1989 it organized the First Global Convention of People of Indian origin in New York City. It was attended by Indians from all over the world and discussed the issues of ethnic image and representations but could not reach any decision.

Besides Pan-Indian organizations, there are a number of social and cultural organizations of Indians which remind the Indians of their ethnic identity. Most of these organizations are formed on the basis of language and/or region. The number of associations coincided with the increase in migration of Indians. For instance in 1960, there was one amalgamating association for the four states of South India, namely Kerala, Tamil Nadu, Karnataka and Andhra Pradesh. But by 1975, people from each of these states formed their own organizations. The speakers of Tulu, one of the languages spoken in Karnataka, were keen to form their own organization but could not do so in 1975, as at that time their number was not sufficiently large to ensure viability of separate identity (Fisher, 1980: 182).

In 1975, there were eleven Indian associations based on common home state/language in New York City alone. There were four associations namely Gujarati, Kannada, Telugu, and

Sindhi which were formed on the basis of natal language. These were formed as "Fellow natal language speakers are thought to share a common culture. The culture referred to was largely bound up with ideas about food habits; what a group typically eats, how the food is prepared, even the physical ways in which it is partaken. ...In fact, it has become clear that the differences between the cognitive categories Punjabi, Bengali, Tamil, and Gujarati have as much to do with food as they do with language" (Fisher, 1980: 180-81). There are seven associations which are named on the basis of their home state. These are Bengal, Bihar, Goa, Kerala, Maharashtra, Rajasthan, and Tamil Nadu. These associations organize monthly or bimonthly programmes that are attended by large number of people. Various programmes are offered in the meetings varying from presentation of dramas, showing of a film, musical performances and even talks from visitors from the home state. These associations also sponsor celebrations of religious festivals such as Diwali. Annual picnics are also arranged by these associations. One important feature of these organizations is that in all such gatherings the food served is typically indigenous of that particular state. Such occasions also provide an opportunity to members to renew their relationships. Thus, such associations play a significant role in maintaining ethnic identity, and the children get exposed to the culture of the home state. Irrespective of their educational and occupational background people participate in large numbers in the activities of these organizations. It has also been observed that "those who have been in this country the longest and are married to non-Indians are most active in all Indian regional associations.... The regional associations serve the purpose of maintaining a separate Indian identity, plus providing a setting for people coming from the same region who also speak the same language" (Saran and Leonard-Spark, 1980: 165). These regional associations also provide a forum for making personal friends and develop social contacts with one another. These associations also provide platform to the members to establish personal relationships and develop a network system. In fact, the networking among the members of regional associations are stronger and more prevalent. Other way of developing social network is through informal contacts. "The owner of a grocery store, or a travel agent, or an insurance agent has direct contact with many members of the community and often serves as a link between those who themselves may lack direct contact and hence support and maintain their identities through such networks" (*ibid.*: 165).

Besides these associations there are "India Clubs" in many university campuses. By participating in the activities of the India club the Indian youth develop positive feeling towards one's Indian background. "India Clubs" are university-affiliated organizations which encourage interaction between students of Indian origin. The activities of these clubs are both social and cultural. They also organize dance programmes and parties and invite dignitaries to lectures on India. The needs of Indian students in the United States especially of newly arrived from India are also met in these clubs. In fact, there are separate organizations for those Indian students who directly come from India. The main reason for their increased affinity with Indian background is due to the fact, that "others" identify them as Indians, regardless of the way they perceive themselves. In other words, it can be said that they have been forced to do so by "others". Thus a distinction is made between "we" and "they".

Religions Activities

The foundation of Hinduism in America was laid in 1890 with the establishment of Ramakrishna Mission by Swami Vivekananda. It was further strengthened by the formation of the *International Society for Krishna Consciousness* (ISKCON) and building temple complexes all over America. Various Hindu festivals such as *Ram Navami*, *Janmashtmi*, *Shivratri* and *Durga Puja* are celebrated at these complexes in which a large number of Hindus in America participate. The number of religious organizations mushroomed with the increase in number of Indians. People belonging to different religious sects preferred to form their own associations.

In the beginning, the Hindus used to invite many well-known and revered religious leaders from India to visit various cities and deliver speeches to preach the religion. Out of such activities emerged Hindu temple societies. These societies took initiative for building temples in various cities. They built temples in New York, Pittsburgh and at times in places that were a little far-off from the cities. It was from mid 1980s that Indians started buying land for constructing temples. Earlier they bought Church buildings and converted them into temples. Sculptors were either called from India for making idols of gods and goddesses or they got them made in India and imported to the States. Besides constructing a sanctum sanctorum where the idols of gods and goddesses were placed for worship, these temple building also have an eating place and a small library and a reading room. Ram Mandir near Chicago, Shiv temple near Los Angeles, and Swaminarayan temple in New York are quite famous. First single temple of Lord Murugan was opened in Washington DC in May 1999. Most of the temples in America have idols of various Hindu gods and goddesses.

Sikhs religious organizations, among Indians in America, are the most highly organized. They have established Gurdwaras where services are held at least once a week, and on all major festivals. They also emphasize maintaining the sanctity of the Sikh religion through observable symbolic representations of their religion which includes turban, steel bangles and the beard. For congregational worship generally three steps are followed by Sikhs. After settling down at the new place they look for other Sikh families in the vicinity. Once a group is formed congregational worship begins and each family offers their residence for the purpose. At the end of the worship meal cooked in Punjabi style is served to all those who are present. As the number of families increases they look for a place where a Gurdwara may be built. Donations are collected for building. All Sikh families also keep religious book called *Granth Sahib* at home which is a collection of sacred hymns which are recited regularly (Nandan and Eames, 1980).

Out of eighty Gurdwaras in America, about 37 per cent are located in California and another four in New Jersey. The first Gurdwara in USA was built in Stockton, California in 1915 after the founding of the Pacific Khalsa Diwan Society in 1912. At that time it was more symbolic than pragmatic assistance to

Sikhs. Since there was no trained *granthi* the service were performed by literate persons by rotation. As the Sikhs were marrying Mexican women the children born to the union had no understanding of their father's cultural or religious background. The majority of the children were marrying non-East Indians. "The *sangat* (congregation) in Stockton gurdwara were largely clean-shaven, sat on chairs, and ate the *karah prasad* (communal sacrament) from paper plates with plastic spoons. The rigid and uncompromising *rahats* (injunctions or code of behaviour) of the Khalsa were looked upon as unnecessary and antiquated by many Sikhs who by 1947 had lived more than half their lives outside India" (La Brack, 1980, 224). Until 1940 Gurdwara was also used by the Punjabi Muslim labourers travelling through Stockton and were allowed to perform their prayers. The arrival of orthodox Sikhs after the relaxation in Immigration policy in 1947 that the tenor of the community changed. With the increase in number of new immigrants "...the question of Sikh identity became increasingly associated with, orthodox Punjabi behavioural norms and Khalsa religious practices. (*ibid*.: 227). Before the arrival of orthodox immigrants "for fifty years, life-cycle rites, with the exception of funerals, were rarely performed there as there were no Punjabi couples who needed marriages performed, few children requiring naming ceremonies, and a few *pahul* initiations requested. The majority of the Punjabi's American born children were raised Catholic. Few Sikhs maintained the turban and beard" (La Brack, 1999: 377).

The attitude of Indian immigrants towards religion has become more favourable since emigration because "religion also serves social and cultural purposes" (Saran and Leonard Spark, 1980: 172). In order to socialize the child in their traditional way of life and also to inculcate traditional values and attitudes, some parents suitably modify their own behaviour and attitudes. In fact, some of the parents participate in religious functions and visit temples and Gurdwaras for the sake of children, as they want to reinforce religious values of their parent culture among them. The married couples more actively participate in religious activities as compared to unmarried members of the community (*ibid.*). The participation in religious activities of immigrants enhances when they have teenagers at home. Since most of the parents of the subcontinent are afraid of peer group pressures on their children regarding dating, marriage, drugs, alcohol and familial relations, they accelerate their participation in the activities of religious organizations in order to expose their children to their own culture. In fact, it has been observed by many scholars that Indians settled in America have become more religious as compared to Indians living in India.

Sometimes the religious functions are combined with social occasions to reinforce their primordial identity. On their visits to India most of the Indians buy religious story books to bring back to the States; these contain stories about various deities such as Shiva, Ganesh, Ram and Krishna; *Panchtantra* stories are other favourites amongst the NRIs. Most of the Indians, specially Hindus, Jains and Sikhs, keep a special place for worship in their homes. Some of them have made replica of temples in their homes to keep images and idols of deities. They have also formed their social and religious organizations and set up temple trusts. The building of *Akshardham* temples in several cities in the United States is a case in point.

Contacts with Parent Culture (India)

Indians even after settling abroad always remain in contact with their relatives and friends in India. Their decision to apply for American citizenship also depend upon family considerations. By adopting American citizenship it is easier for them to help their kith and kin to migrate to USA. The new arrivals from India did not feel strangers in a new country because of the presence of their relatives who had already settled there. The family networks are extensive and it is quite common to have all of their primary relatives and in some cases even secondary relatives in USA. This networking also plays significant role in the adjustment of new arrivals in the new environment who are provided all help including financial. When they visit India most of the times their visits are mainly confined to the villages, city, or region of origin. The adaptation of the traits of the host culture would depend on the consistency and frequency with which contact and communication with family in India are maintained (Angelo, 1997).

Majority of the first generation people maintain their ties with people back in India, by paying regular visits on various occasions. Among second generation, especially those who had never visited India, know about India through American Television which always shows negative side of Indian life and culture. Even those second generation children who have been to India had mixed feelings. Their main concern is that when they visit India, people do not appreciate their American accent and consider them as Americans. In USA, the Americans call them Indians and do not accept them as part of the mainstream. Thus, the second generation people are "sandwiched" between the two, and they develop a feeling of alienation. They consider themselves in no man's land, that they are neither here nor there. "...while in the United States, they do not feel completely American, and while in India, they do not feel genuinely Indian" (Agarwal, 1991: 43). The second generation call themselves as Indians and Americans in different ways. Being born and raised in America they have exposed to American education, identity, and philosophy and majority of their friends are American and therefore they identify themselves as American. But being of Indian descent and brought up with Indian values and beliefs they are also Indian (Sheth, 2001). Thus these people are really sandwiched between the two cultures.

Before the information technology revolution, communications with relatives and friends was done through letters and occasionally through telephones as facilities in India were limited. But the IT revolution has altered the entire scenario. Now communication through letters have become obsolete and has been replaced by telephones, both landline as well as mobiles, and internet. Chatting through internet with your friends and relatives in any part of the world has become common affair. By installing web camera in your computer one can also watch live action of the other party. Recently when we visited a friend in Gurgaon they were watching the live movements of their six months old grandchild in America.

These developments have abridged the gaps and have strengthened the family ties and weaken the chances of integration.

Through social networking Punjabis and Gujaratis in USA have maintained their relations with their kith and kin all around the world including India. Through this network they not only send remittances but are also involved in many national and international organizations. All this has been facilitated with the development in information technology. Punjabis have developed two levels of social network; one with the relatives back home and other with the Punjabis all over the globe. Punjabis help their family members in improving their financial status by sending money which is used in buying land and establishing business such as transport companies. They also contribute in development work such as building schools and hospitals. Kinship ties are also kept alive either visiting Indian or inviting family members to USA, though the frequency of visit varies from person to person. Some visit more often whereas there are others who visit on some occasions. Regarding their return to India, majority have no plans to return.

Like Punjabis, Gujarati have also developed transnational network through which they remain in touch with their relatives in Indian and with other Gujarati in USA and in other countries. Gujarati network also works at two levels. The personalized and informal linkages which can be maintained through telephones, internet and personal visits have been classified in micro level. Through this they are able to remain in touch with fellow Gujarati in India and in other countries. These links are maintained in the form of marital relations, kinship network, remittances and religious activities (Gopa Kumar, 2003). The linkages between Gujarati diaspora and the mother country and among the diaspora community in other countries have been put in the category of macro level. Besides maintaining contact with the Government of India and the Government of Gujarat for developmental activities, they have also established international associations and organizations. Through these associations and organizations Gujarati interact with Gujarati all over the world (Gopa Kumar, 2003). Gujarati have also developed websites through which they are creating global directories of individuals, community associations and business organizations owned by Gujarati diaspora community.

Watching Indian movies and listening to Indian music have also become passion with migrants from India. Earlier they used to watch movies through VCR but now CD's are commonly used. Even the CD of those movies not yet released in India are available there. This has been confirmed in personal communication by number of NRI's while they were visiting India. Children are also exposed to regional culture and language through mass media. Indians also regularly subscribe to magazines from India, listen to Indian music, and also watch Indian movies on Television (Saran and Leonard-Spark, 1980). There are few Indians who like American music whereas majority prefer Indian music.

Indian remix music and dance is the most popular sub-culture visible and audible among Indian American youth. Hindi film music and *Bhangra* have been remixed with American rap, techno, jungle and reggae and this has become part of the broader popular culture. This remix first emerged in mid 1980s among British Born South Asian youth and since then has travelled to New York, Delhi, Bombay, Toronto, Port of Spain, etc. One significant feature of this remix is that though it emerged among urban areas, but its expressions are shaped by local context (Maira, 2002: 29-30). The parties where this remix music is played are attended even by those youth who had not been to college. "The music is remixed or at least selected by deejays, who perform at parties hosted at local clubs, restaurants, and college campuses by promoters, generally young Indian men and women, some of whom are college students who do this as a source of part-time income and who have helped create an urban South Asian American youth sub-culture" (*ibid.*: 31). These parties are advertised through word of mouth, mailing lists, websites and flyers distributed in stores, clubs and other places visited by youth. These parties are arranged every weekend and attended by Indian youth from New York, New Jersey, Connecticut and Pennsylvania. Such an event also "...displays the construction of a culturally hybrid style, such as Indian-style nose rings and bindis with nip-hop clothing and performing ethnic identity through dance" (*ibid.*: 32).

Thus continuous interaction with friends and relatives back in India and exposure to Indian culture through movies have curtailed the chances of integration and assimilation in the host society and in all probability they will be sandwiched between the two cultures.

Summary of the Aperture opening and insulatory mechanisms which facilitate or hinder the process of assimilation and integration of Indians in the United States are listed below:

Aperture Openings

(i) Intermarriage (Breakdown of endogamy)

In the beginning of migration some Sikhs married Mexican women but later on they divorced them and maintained their endogamy. By and large those who came after 1965 married within caste. Very few cases of marriages between Indians and Americans are there.

(ii) Adoption of names of the host society

Some people shorten their names as Americans were not able to pronounce their names. But majority did not change their names.

(iii) Adoption of the language

Early migrants from Punjab were uneducated farmers who lived on their ranches and had limited interaction with the locals. They did not learn the language but encouraged their children to learn English. Later migrants who were professionals already knew the language as English is one of the medium of instruction in India especially at the higher level. The teaching of English in India starts at the lower level.

(iv) Religious conversion

Indians in America did not change their religion. All of them not only followed their religious beliefs but also promoted it by opening temples and Gurdwaras.

(v) Adoption of food habits and developing taste for host cuisine

Younger generation of Indians developed taste for host cuisine but the older generation by and large preferred to have Indian food. In most of the houses Indian food is served and that too with regional flavour.

Insulatory Mechanisms

(i) Retention of mother tongue

Except some younger generation people who use American English, majority use their mother tongue. At home it is the mix of English and the mother tongue. Steps are also taken by all Indians to promote the regional languages.

(ii) Concentration in certain living quarters

There is no definite pattern of residential pattern of Indians except early migrants who stayed close to each other.

(iii) Separate educational facilities

Except making arrangements for teaching of mother tongue, Indians are sending their children to American schools. Since the educational facilities in American institutions are excellent no separate educational institutions are required.

(iv) Endogamy

In the beginning of migration of Indians in America, some Sikhs married Mexican women. There are few cases of inter caste marriages but by and large Indians have preferred to marry within caste.

(v) Concentration in certain occupations

No definite pattern of occupations have been adopted by Indians in America. Depending upon the circumstances they have selected their occupations. Majority of the Gujaratis and Sikhs have given preference to business which may vary from grocery to travel agency.

(vi) Voluntary organizations

All Indians have formed their regional organizations to promote their cultural and religious practices. Through these activities they keep the parent culture alive which reduces their chances of assimilation. These activities are held in regional languages a platform is provided to younger generation to learn the language.

(vii) Parental religion

Besides pursuing their religious activities steps are also taken to promote it. The construction of religious temples and also worshiping at homes the religion is kept alive. By and large Indians do not change their religion.

(viii) Continuation of food habits and taboos

All Indians except few younger generation stick to their Indian food and continue with the taboos.

(ix) Cultural diacriticals

There is not much difference in the dressing pattern of all males except Sikhs who can be identified by their physical diacriticals of turban and beard. Some Sikhs have cut their hair short but when they visit India they wear turban. At home Indian males may use their regional outfit. Ladies, by and large wear their traditional dress but working women and young ones use jeans and skirts.

(x) Contact with parent culture

Indians in America always remain in touch with their friends and relatives either visiting India or inviting them to USA. They also take help of their relatives to find a suitable match for their wards. Revolution in information technology has brought the Indians abroad closer to parent culture. Through internet, e-mails and mobiles they have not lost the contact. The availability of Indian films on DVD they can watch even the latest movies sitting in their drawing rooms. Even the young generation are also exposed to Indian culture by all these means.

The insulatory mechanisms operating in foreign country have reduced the chances of Indian to assimilate in the host society.

Summing Up

The early migrants, especially Punjabis, from India to the United States of America maintained their separate identity and resisted absorption into the mainstream. Except for a short period when they were marrying Mexican women they maintained separate identity and a shared sense of people hood. They were particular in adhering to their cultural norms, putting pressure on their young children to uphold Punjabi Sikh values and customs, and at the same time they were receptive to change and ready to learn new ways from other groups. Their strategy of accommodation without assimilation helped them maintain their separate identity.

Most of the Indian parents show real concern for their children. Parents like some of the characteristics of American culture but they do not appreciate when children start questioning them for every thing. In fact, a derogatory term *American Born Confused Desi* or "ABCD" has been used for Indian youth as they face identity crisis. Some of the young people call themselves as "coconuts—brown on the outside, white on the inside" (Agarwal, 1991: 34). This situation arises as the parents of young people would like their children to have two identities, both as Indians as well as Americans. While comparing Indian youth with other Asian groups Agarwal points out that "The Indian culture maintains a more severe taboo on openness in pre-marital, male-female relationships. Dating is not an institution in India, as marriages are traditionally arranged by one's family.... Another way in which Indians differ from other Asians is in their inability to assimilate into American society on a religious level" (*ibid.*: 36). One complaint most of the youth make against their parents is that they use the same standards with which they themselves grew up in India over 25 years ago without realizing that conditions have changed even in India.

The younger generation people appreciate the family values of Indians and the closeness is considered as the essence of Indianness. They also like the religion as well as many customs and traditions of India. But majority did not approve the caste system or social stratification. Some of the other characteristics of Indians which are criticized by the second generation includes rigid food habits and attitude towards women and so many rituals. According to them it is their social attitude and religious beliefs that did not allow them to integrate in mainstream America (Agarwal, 1991 and Sheth, 2001).

While the first generation people were more inclined to associate with individuals from the same region due to language and customs, the younger generation people do not have such preference. Majority of them prefer to have friends of mixed international background. Since the second generation people are more exposed to non-Indians either in school or at the place of work, they have better chances of assimilation into mainstream American society. These people also do not like the perpetuation of regionalism and sectionalism, the attitude adopted by their parents. They would prefer to have Pan-Indian identity rather than promoting regionalism. On the whole the younger generation people born and brought up in USA would prefer to have "dual culture", what Atal has called "Sandwich Culture". It was felt by most of them that "they need to be given the sense that they are both Indian and American, not Indian guests in a foreign land" (Agarwal, 1991: 60). They want to absorb positive culture of both the societies. "The young Indian is determined, studious, focused, and family oriented, while the young American is self-confident, independent and well-rounded" (*ibid.*: 60). Some of the teenagers remarked that they were born in USA as their parents choose to migrate. As they had no choice they have every right to be a part of the mainstream. (Sheth, 2001).

Indian American youth have really been "sandwiched" by having multiple identities moving between family and school. Among peers they wear baggy pants and earrings but at jobs they change to conservative attire and at home they become dutiful daughters and sons. Second generation youth are also exposed to Indian values and customs by participating in various functions organized by regional, linguistic and geographical organizations. Through these activities they are vicariously socialized into various sub-cultures of the group, as these regional identifications have assumed greater significance among Indians in America. As compared to these second generation Indians, the cultural conditions of early immigrants from India did not allow them to have much interaction with the Americans and in the process they were alienated from the mainstream. The Indians who came after 1965 were more open towards American culture but they were also not ready to compromise with their traditional values and beliefs.

Robert Park and the Chicago Sociologists had predicted a race-relation cycle of "contact, accommodation, assimilation, and ultimate amalgamation of ethnic groups through inter-racial marriages and social interaction across generations" (Maira, 2002: 90). However, this "melting pot" model was challenged during the civil war of 1960s and 1970s by pluralistic theories. Their main argument was that ethnic groups would continue to maintain their identities in later generations. This "Salad Bowl" approach was an improvement over the ethnocentrism of melting pot, but it did not take into account the historical inequalities between ethnic groups. In 1980s and 1990s, attempts were made to analyze social and historical determinants as well as situations-specific ethnic identification.

Researches on post 1965 immigrants have suggested a model of "segmented assimilation", proposing that different groups of second generation youth enter different economic sectors and sub-cultures in American society (*ibid*.: 90-91). Those second generation youth who did not have access to these ethnic organizations use other sources such as Jackson Heights, where restaurants and stores sell South Asian food products, music, cloths and publications from India. To maintain their ethnic identity, many second generation youth wear ethnic clothing and attend celebrations of Indian festivals.

CHAPTER-4

Punjabis and Gorakhpuris in Thailand

Cultural contact between the people of India and the countries of South East Asia[11] were established long before but it was during Mauryan period between 330 B.C. and 180 B.C. that Indian culture and religion left their imprint. This was the beginning of the Indianization of the region. The process was enhanced when large number of Brahmans from Kalinga in Orissa migrated and settled in the region. The massacre by Emperor Asoka forced them to abandon their home. Migrants from South India also contributed substantially to the early phases of India's cultural influence in Southeast Asia especially during Pallavas (230 B.C. to 225 A.D.) and the Cholas (First A.D. onwards) period. The process of Indianization got further boost from the first century A.D. when some Indian migrants founded their own kingdom by marrying the daughters of the local chieftains. The adoption of brahmanical rites and ceremonies and the use of Sanskrit language by the rulers led to the spread of Hinduism in the region. This has been well documented by the archaeologists on the basis of inscriptions, coins and other material found during excavation. However, with the spread of Buddhism in the later centuries led to the decline of Hinduism. Buddhism was promoted in the region by Emperor Asoka who sent his son and daughter to preach Buddhism. Now Buddhism is the main religion in the region.

The presence of Indian cultural elements in the societies of Southeast Asia bears testimony to the long history of cultural contacts between India and these countries. The migrating Indians assimilated with the local people; some of them marrying the locals. They were, thus, able to influence the culture of the local people, but in the process they lost their own identity. The best example of such people are the Oriya Brahmins in Thailand. They live in a Hindu temple in Bangkok, and are known as Thai Brahmins. They have married local Thai ladies, speak only Thai language, eat Thai food and act as priests at the royal ceremonies; their being descendants of Oriya migrants is relegated to history. It is also important to mention that the Thai king took help of Oriya priests in devising a script for Thai language. Most of the letters in the Thai script bear resemblance to Oriya script. The script itself is called "Thepnagari"—a derivative of Devnagari used for Sanskrit and Hindi scripts.

Some remnants of Indian culture especially in literature, festivals, and religion can still found in Thai society. Thai vocabulary is based on Sanskrit language. Names of human beings, cities, towns, provinces, trees, plants, flowers, months and days in Thai language clearly show the influence of Sanskrit (Shastri, 1982). For instance, the Sanskrit words for god and goddess are *deva* and *devi* which are pronounced as *thepa* and *thepi* in Thai. For a friend Sanskrit word is *Mitra* and in Thai it is called *Mit*. The names of disciplines in Thai also show impact of Sanskrit. The disciplines which end with logy in English are named as *vidaya* in Thai, while those ending with *ics* are termed as *sat*, which is a derivative of Sanskrit sastra. Anthropology in Thai is called as *Manusyavidya* (Manusya means man in Sanskrit) and Logic is called Takavidya in Thai which is derived from Sanskrit word tark. These are just few illustrations but Thai language is full of Sanskrit words.

There are two festivals in Thailand, namely Loi Krathong (festival of lights) and Song Kran (a derivative of Sanskrit word Sankranti)(water splashing frestival) which reminds the festival of Deepwali and Holi in India. However, the purpose and celebrations are altogether different. The festival of lights in Thailand is celebrated in November by making rafts of plantain stems which are decorated with flags, paper umbrellas, incense sticks and lighted candles with offerings of food and flowers. At dusk these rafts are made to float in the river. It is a belief that candle in each raft represents a wish. The water splashing festival known as *Songkran* is celebrated on April 13 every year.

It is celebrated as a new year and on this day they wash the images of Buddha in the temples and sprinkle the cented water on friends and relatives.

The people of Thailand have also been influenced by one of the great epics of Hindus, the *Ramayana*. In Thailand, *Ramayana* is known as *Ramakriti*; and it has been indigenised by the Thais. They have adapted it according to their ways of life and it portrays the customs and beliefs of Thai people. Dresses of the characters have also been altered accordingly. Santosh Desai (1980) who has compared the Thai version of *Ramayana* with that of Valmiki, found that some of the characters are same whereas a few differ. There are few characters in Thai Ramayana which do not appear in Valmiki Ramayana. The Valmiki Ramayana has seven parts whereas Thai Ramayana is one continuous story. There are certain episodes which are totally different from that of Valmiki.

Above description reveals that the Indians who migrated to Southeast Asia were able to transmit some of their culture and religion which were incorporated and adopted by the local people. Though they succeeded in transmitting some of their cultural traits, yet were also influenced by the local culture. Gradually, Indians who migrated during this period assimilated in the local culture of the region. This was the first wave of migration to Southeast Asia including Thailand.

History of Migrations of Indians Currently in Thailand

The second wave of Indian migration to Thailand began sometime in 19th century when the British were granted permission to trade at Thailand's port in 1826. The signing of the Bowring Treaty in 1855 and fourteen more treaties in the next fifteen years with other trading nations of Europe converted the self-sufficient economy of Thailand into a dual economy, "one part traditional and the other increasingly commercialized. The latter produced agricultural raw materials and materials for a world market, receiving in exchange Western manufactured goods" (Girling, 1981: 45). Under the Bowring Treaty, the foreigners were granted territoriality and the British subjects were given the right to trade freely in all seaports and to reside permanently in Bangkok. This encouraged the British protected subjects like Burmese, and Indians to migrate to Thailand. The declaration that Indians in any part of the British empire had equal rights to those of any other of Her Majesty's subjects (Queen of England) helped them to established trading and commercial centres in Thailand.

The complete abolition of slavery in 1905 in Thailand resulted in an acute shortage of labour supply. Since the local Thais were not prepared to work as hired labourers in plantations (rubber and teak) and in mining activities, Indian and Chinese immigrants filled the gap. This did not create any conflict with the native population as they preferred to work in rice cultivation rather than on plantations. The King of Thailand allowed the employment of foreigners including Indians, in various government agencies.

Tamilians, both Hindus and Muslims, were the first group of Indians to come to Thailand sometime in the 19th century. The educated Tamilians were employed by the British firms, whereas Tamil Muslims were engaged as butchers. There were other Tamilians who traded precious stones. The fourth group of Tamils worked as labourers to construct railway line between Penang and Bangkok. There was another group of Muslims who also came to Bangkok almost at the same time from Surat and Bombay. These people were known as Bohras and were in textile business. There were about 10-15 families of Bohra Muslims, and the number of Tamil families was around fifty.

Punjabis started migrating to Thailand in 1884 AD and in the beginning there were about 20 families of Punjabis and all of them were concentrated in the Phaurat area only. Kirparam Madan from Bhadewal village in Sialkot district (now in Pakistan) who was a Sehajdhari Sikh was the first to migrate to Thailand. Later on, his wife's family who was from a Narula family of village Philloke in Gujaranwala district (now in Pakistan) followed. All of them were engaged in textile business. Gradually, their number increased. In the beginning, the Punjabis of three districts of the then Western Punjab (now Pakistan), namely Gujaranwala, Sekhopura and Sialkot migrated to Thailand. All of them belonged to the Arora caste and three sub-castes, namely Madan, Narula and Chawla. In 1890, the brothers of Kirparam's wife started their own firm called Messers Bhagwan Singh and Company in the name of their father. Later on they were joined by their other brothers and their families and within a few years they became one of the richest firms in Thailand. All the descendants of these brothers at present are successful businessmen of Thailand. Kirparam who had his own business also brought his sons. The grandsons of Kirparam are having their own businessmen in Bangkok. Another Punjabi family to migrate to Thailand was the family of the brother of the father of Kirparam's wife. Gradually, other Sikh families of village Philloke migrated to Thailand and by 1910 large number of Punjabis, both Sikhs and Hindus had settled in Thailand. At that time no distinction was made among Hindus and Sikhs. It was a common practice for a family to offer one of the sons to Sikhism. Most of the Punjabi migrants of that time were related to each other. All of them belonged to Arora caste and three sub-castes, namely Madan, Narula and Chawla.

Gorakhpuris also started migrating to Thailand around the late 19th century. Some Gorakhpuris went to Burma after the First War of Indian Independence in 1857 due to fear of prosecution by the British for their role in the revolt. Being a part of India, Burma was not considered a safe place, therefore these people decided to migrate to Thailand. Initially, there were about 20 families of Gorakhpuris and all of them were dairymen. Since the atmosphere in Thailand was congenial, they decided to settle there and gradually brought their families and other relatives.

Large number of Punjabis and Gorakhpuris migrated during the Second World War. There were quite a few army personnel who were fighting for the British in Malaysia and Singapore and were disgusted by the discriminatory behaviour of the British officers in matters of promotion and other facilities. Some of these officers deserted the British army and joined hands with Indian revolutionaries to form the Indian Independence League, which later on was redesignated as the Indian National Army.

At that time Bangkok was the centre of the Indian Independence League.

No official record exists about the actual number of Indians currently living in Thailand. The Directory of Siam published in 1921 showed that there were 20,769 Indians in Thailand. Namporia as quoted by Zakir Hussain (1982) mentions 25,000 Indians in 1967. In March 1989, a business in Thailand special report released at the inauguration ceremony of the Fair Trade of the Indian Industrial exhibition mentions over 65,000 people of Indian origin in Thailand, and about 90 per cent of these people stay in Bangkok. However, for the last few years Indians have started penetrating in large numbers to the countryside also. Punjabis, both Sikhs and non-Sikhs as well as people from Uttar Pradesh (popularly known as Gorakhpuris) constitute 50 and 40 per cent of the total Indian population respectively, in Bangkok. The remaining 10 per cent are Tamils, Muslims, Rajasthanis, Gujaratis and Sindhis.

Hindus of Bangkok numbering about forty thousand are divided in various groups. On the basis of language and their region of origin in India, they can be identified as Gorakhpuris, Gujaratis, Marwaris, Punjabis, Sindhis and Tamilians. Of all these groups, Punjabis and Gorakhpuris constitute about 80 per cent of the total Hindus. In this chapter we have concentrated on the cultural adaptation of Sikhs and Hindus (both Punjabis and Gorakhpuris) in Thai society.

Pattern of Migration

Sikhs came to Thailand to settle down permanently. There are few who first came alone and later on brought their families. Another category is of those who came as bachelors; some of them got married here whereas few went back to India for marriage. Chain migration was the dominant pattern among Sikhs as one member of the family was followed by others and in few years the entire consanguineal relations migrated to Thailand. In few cases even the affinal relations also migrated and settled in Thailand. There are few cases of self-inspired migration.

The pattern of migration of Hindu Punjabis is similar to that of Sikhs. Like Sikhs, Hindu Punjabis also followed the chain pattern of migration; one member of the family being followed by other members. Among Hindu Punjabis, like Sikhs, it is rare to find any case of relay migration, though in recent years some cases of self-inspired migration can be found.

There are many Punjabi families who have been living in Thailand for the last four or more generations. Among the old migrants, the majority are permanent residents, though a few have taken Thai citizenship. Younger generation among Hindu Punjabis and Sikhs have opted for Thai citizenship but the old people preferred to retain their Indian nationality. Some of them are naturalized citizen of Thailand. Most of the Hindu Punjabis either migrated with their families or brought them later on. Very few cases of single migrants were noticed.

Among Gorakhpuris relay migration is the dominant pattern. Those who migrated in the beginning have been replaced by their brothers and/or sons. There are very few cases of chain migration and self-inspired migration. A large number of Gorakhpuris have not brought their "families" and are living alone. This was and still is the prominent feature of Gorakhpuris. However, some of them bring their families for brief visits, especially during the summer holidays of children. These people visit India at regular intervals to meet their kinsfolk. There are cases where grown up children, especially the girls have been sent to India for studies or for matrimony. It is important to note that while these people lead a frugal life here, they save substantial sums of money to remit to India where it is used to enhance their family status with such indicators as: purchase of tractors, purchase of additional land, building pucca house, and better education and standard of living of children.

The majority of the Gorakhpuris are not in favour of acquiring Thai citizenship. Most of them are staying as permanent residents; only a few have opted for Thai citizenship. There are a large number of Gorakhpuris who are staying in Thailand as temporary migrants for years together. These people visit Malaysia or India after the expiry of three months (the period for which their visa is valid) and re-enter getting fresh visas.

Indians in Thailand can be classified in two categories. In the first category are those who migrated because their kins were already there and the second category is that of self-inspired migrants. Among Punjabis it is chain migration as one member followed other members and gradually the entire kin group settled in Thailand. The common pattern among Gorakhpuris is relay migration as only one member migrated at a time. There are very few cases of chain migration among Gorakhpuris. Self-inspired migrants can be found among Punjabis as well among Gorakhpuris. All Indians in Thailand can be classified in the following categories:

1. **Period of Migration:** This includes (a) early migrants like Oriya and Tamil Brahmins, whose history of migration is not known. They have assimilated in Thai society. (b) Migrants who came in the beginning of the 19th century. These are of two types (i) those who have assimilated in Thai society and (ii) those who have retained their Indianness. (c) Those who came between 1900 and the Second World War. (d) Those who migrated during India's Independence struggle. (e) Those who came during and after partition of India.
2. **Length of Stay:** Depending on the length of stay in Thailand, Indians can be classified as (i) those who are living for the last four or more generation, (ii) those who are living for the last three generation, (iii) those who are in Thailand for the last two generation, and (iv) first generation migrants.
3. **Status of Migrants:** Status-wise Indians can be classified as (i) permanent migrants who have become Thai citizen and those who have retained Indian citizenship. (ii) Temporary migrants are those who are living in Thailand for many years but after every three months they leave the country and reenter with fresh visa (temporary migrants get visa for three months).
4. **Pattern of Migration:** This includes (a) who migrated along with their family, (b) who came alone and brought their family later on, (c) those who never brought their

family and (d) those whose family visits Thailand for short duration.

5. **Reasons for Migration:** Both pull and push factors have influenced the migration. This includes (a) for financial gain, (b) partition of India, and (c) encouraged by relatives.

Settlement Pattern

Concentration of Indians in different parts of Bangkok is easily noticeable. A market-cum-residential area called Phaurat is also known as mini-India. Besides cheaper boarding and lodging available for visitors from Indian sub-continent, the area has a number of shops catering to the needs of the visitors from India and Pakistan. Quite a few Indian families, both Punjabis and Gorakhpuris reside in Phaurat. About three to four kilometres from the Phaurat, across the river is Thonburi, where many Indian families reside. Earlier majority of Indians both Hindus and Sikhs were residing here but now some prosperous Indians, particularly Punjabis both Sikhs and non-Sikhs—have moved to the newly developed Sukhumvit area. Still there are quite a large number of Indians who live in Thonburi. There are two streets in Thonburi unofficially known as Nanak Villa and Gobind Villa, where about 200 Sikh families stay. A large number of Gorakhpuri also stay in the Thonburi area. Sukhumvit is a long road which has, many bye lanes, known as Soi in Thai, on both sides. A large number of Indians are settled in some of these bye lanes. In some lanes, there is concentration of Indians. For instance, in Sukhumvit Soi 70 about 150-200 families of Namdhari Sikhs live. Other Soi where there is a large concentration of Indians mainly Punjabis are 39 and 49. The area around Oriental Hotel is mainly inhabited by Muslims. Opposite Indira Hotel in Pratunam number of Namdhari Sikh families stay. Gorakhpuris also live in large numbers near Vishnu Mandir at 50 Thung Wat Don Yanuawa. Thus, we find that Indians are spread all over Bangkok but in some areas their concentration is more. One prominent feature of the settlement pattern is that except in Phaurat, areas of concentration of Punjabis and Gorakhpuris are different. In Phaurat one can find mixed population of Punjabis and Gorakhpuris. Most of the Gorakhpuris belong to the middle and lower class, they cannot afford to live in the area inhabited by the rich. They have a tendency to congregate and reside together in a common area. There is a concentration of Gorakhpuris in Thonburi and around the Vishnu temple.

Vocational Activities

Indians in Bangkok are engaged in various types of vocations, but majority of them are self-employed, engaged in some kind of business, small or big. Some of the occupations in which Indians are engaged include textiles, precious stones, import and export, travel agency, hoteliering, tailoring, watchman, newspaper distributors, nut/bread hawking and dairying. There are few occupations such as that of watchman, milkman, newspaper distributor and hawker which are generally pursued by Gorakhpuris. Punjabis are engaged mostly in textiles, hoteliering and tailoring and import and export. Details of their vocations are discussed in this section.

The establishment of European and British commercial and business firms in Thailand in the 20th century provided job opportunities to many immigrants. All foreign companies till 1950's used to hire Indians, especially Gorakhpuris as watchmen because of their rudimentary knowledge of the English language and their honest nature. Gorakhpuris had their association with strong leadership which used to serve as employment agency. This association provided all sorts of help to their compatriots to get jobs. It worked as a well-organized group. But now Indian watchmen have been replaced by local Thais or Chinese. Well-trained watchmen are supplied by many security agencies which have cropped up after 1950. About 20 Indians were working as watchmen in different branches of a particular bank in Bangkok till November 1981, when services of all of them were terminated with one month's notice (Hussain, 1982). One can still find some Indians working as watchmen, but almost all of them are engaged by Indian business firms. They had a very hard life. Most of these people who are working as watchmen have not brought their wives and children to Bangkok.

Till 1950s the selling of milk and milk products was the monopoly of the Yadavas of Uttar Pradesh. After the introduction of the modern dairy companies, most of the milkmen have given up this occupation as the competition became too tough. Now, there are very few Indian milkmen in Bangkok and they supply milk to a few households and small restaurants.

Some of the Indian people whose services were terminated as watchmen and who had given up the business of selling milk and milk products, took to nut, newspaper and roti hawking. Very often one can come across these hawkers in the various business centres of Bangkok. Since this occupation needs little capital, and lack of knowledge of the Thai language is no obstacle, most of the new migrants from Uttar Pradesh go for such business. According to the late Ayumongol Sonakul, a journalist of repute who used to write regularly in *The Bangkok Post*, a leading daily newspaper of Bangkok, wrote that the Indian nut vendors have become a "part of the Bangkok tradition—an integral part of the city's scenery. He is like what the Chinese noodle-vendor used to be only the Chinese noodle vender has now become Thai, while the Indian nut vendor has not" (*The Bangkok Post*, 26 March 1982). He further adds that "if the Indian stops hawking nuts something will be missing from its traditional scenery" (*ibid.*). Once an Indian vendor was arrested for infringing the Alien's Act. According to this Act, only Thai nationals are permitted to hawk in the streets, the occupation being a reserved one. This law was formulated to protect Thais from the increasing number of Chinese vendors. But Ayumongol argued that "the nut vendor is not depriving any Thai citizen of his job. We have Thais now hawking noodles, but have not ever heard of any Thai at all, even one Thai, who has felt the urge to put a table on his head and go around hawking assorted nuts" (*ibid.*). Gorakhpuris are engaged as sales persons by Sikh and Hindu Punjabis running wholesale and retail businesses of textiles. Some are also working as caretakers of the Guest Houses, owned by Punjabis. There are about 10 Gorakhpuris selling betel leaf.

Till a few years ago, moneylending was one of the very popular occupations among Indians, especially among the

Sikhs. Poor Thai people were their customers. Now, there are very few Sikhs doing this business. Moneylending is a family run business which passes from father to son. Now very few Sikhs are engaged in this business. Risk is also involved in this business. Sometime the customer may disappear and the person may loose his money. One such case was reported by Zakir Hussain (1982). Indians who are engaged in these occupations mostly belong to the lower middle class.

Another occupation which is quite popular among Indians is NGOEN-SOD. In common terminology they call it *Unq-Phong* or ding-dong. Gorakhpuris as well as Punjabis, both the Sikhs and non-Sikhs are engaged in this business. Even some Punjabi women pursue this vocation. In this business, Indians supply various items to local Thais by visiting them at their homes and take payment on a daily instalment basis. For instance, if someone wants to own a colour T.V. and is not in a position to pay the lump sum amount of 6000 Baht, the businessmen will supply the item but will charge almost double this amount, to be paid in daily instalments. The amount to be paid daily can be decided by the parties concerned. Quite a large number of Indians are pursuing this trade (Gupta, 1999).

Majority of the first generation Punjabis, both Sikhs and Hindus, were self-employment, engaged in some kind of business. Some of them are still active but majority have taken retirement due to old age or poor health. In second generation 79 per cent continued in the business whereas 21 per cent became business executive. Among third generation only 14 per cent continued in business, 50 per cent were working as business executive, 8 per cent became government employee and 28 per cent joined semi-government jobs or banks (Hussain, 1982). This shows that over the years the occupational pattern among Indians has changed.

The analysis of the *Telephone Directory of Indian Residents* in Thailand shows that Indians are engaged in wide range of jobs. Out of 1248 persons listed in the directory, it was possible to ascertained the details of 486 Indians. Thailand being a leading country in textiles majority of Indians are connected with textiles and tailoring in one way or other. In 1989 eighteen Indians were the owner of textiles mills. About one-fourth of these were in textile business. Some of them in readymade garments business and quite large number were in tailoring business. In fact, tailoring and textile together account for more than fifty per cent of the Indians. Tailoring was in the hands of Punjabis and Sindhis. Other more popular occupations in which Indians were involved included travel and tour agents, restaurants and guest houses, gem and precious stone business and import and export.

Family and Marriage Pattern

As the families of large number of Gorakhpuris live in India they remain in regular touch with them either visiting India or calling them to Thailand. There are many cases among Gorakhpuris who have sent their grown up children especially the girls to India for studies or for matrimony. Majority of Gorakhpuris in Thailand lead a frugal life and save substantial sum of money to remit to India where it is used to enhance their family status either by purchasing a tractor or additional land and building a *pucca* house. Money thus saved is also used as dowry in the marriage of their daughters.

Gorakhpuris are more traditional as compared to Sikhs and Hindu Punjabis. Children especially the girls submit to their parents' wishes in terms of education and marriage. Boys also listen to their parents as far as marriage is concerned, but for education they may take their own decisions. However, all Gorakhpuris send their children—both boys and girls—to India for education. They are afraid of exposure of their children, especially the girls to the alien culture. Very rarely one may find Gorakhpuri females going alone to the market. They are almost always accompanied by the male members of the family even for a visit to the temple.

Visits to a Gorakhpuri family show no impact of living in a foreign country. Females do all the household work from cleaning to cooking. In all households one can find the photographs of Indian political leaders such as Nehru, Gandhi, Indira Gandhi and Subhas Chandra Bose. Calendars with pictures of various gods and goddesses such as Ram, Krishna, Lakshmi and Hanuman can be seen in every house. Another indicator of maintaining their Indianness is the availability of literature in the form of books and magazines from India. Those who cannot afford to purchase them, borrow from their friends.

All Sikh households keep the photographs of Guru Nanak, Guru Gobind Singh and the Golden Temple at Amritsar. In fact, a Sikh household is a replica of a typical Indian home. Due respect is paid to elders in the family and children are taught to obey their decisions. Till a few years ago, all Punjabis looked towards India for finding mates for their children. Now, in the groups like Sikhs that have a sizeable membership, marriage partners are sought even in Thailand. With increasing wealth, the marriage circle is getting widened in terms of countries from where Sikhs get their affinal kin. Such widening of the circle has not disturbed the religion and caste consideration and even where caste boundaries are transgressed, the deviance does not go beyond the common origin as Indians.

There was a time when Sikhs were sending their girls to settle in India after marriage. Now, the girls, born and brought up in Thailand do not generally want to get married in India for fear of migrating back to India and getting adjusted in strange environs. Sikhs do not generally want their daughters to marry a non-Sikh. They first look for a suitable match in Thailand, failing that they look to neighbouring countries such as Hong Kong, Malaysia and Singapore. The other alternative is to "smuggle" in suitable boys for their daughters who are regularized as immigrants after the marriage.

Once a suitable match is found all the traditional customs of marriage are performed. Marriages of Sikhs are held in Gurdwara and the chief priest called *Granthi* performs all the rites. Even if a court marriage has taken place, it is no substitute for a traditional marriage. Among Sikhs a formal betrothal is not necessary but if both parties want, a mutually agreed day may be fixed for token betrothal when the girl's parents visit the boy's parents and in the presence of *sangat* (congregation) and *Guru Granth Sahib* (Holy Book), the girl's party presents a *kirpan*, a bracelet (*kara*) and some sweets to the boy. No astrologers and horoscopes are consulted for fixing the date of marriage. Any day which is mutually acceptable may be fixed for *Anand karaj* (marriage ceremony). Generally, Sikh marriages are held on Sundays.

Some changes have been noticed in the marriage pattern of Hindu Punjabis. Earlier, they used to select suitable matches from India for their wards, but gradually a change has been noticed. Since it is not easy to get visa, people have started marrying their sons and daughters locally. Hindu Punjabi girls like Sikh girls also resist going to India after marriage. While selecting a spouse for their wards, first preference is given to find a person of the same caste, but failing that they ignore the caste factor. Though we do not have data to confirm this, yet intercaste marriages among them are gradually increasing. All Hindu Punjabis consult a Hindu priest before fixing the marriage of their wards. Some even match the horoscopes of the prospective bride and groom. The date and time of the marriage is also fixed in consultation with the priest. Generally, people consult the chief priest before fixing the marriages of their wards. Most of the marriages in Thailand are solemnized by the chief priest.

No change has been noticed in the marriage pattern of Gorakhpuris. While selecting a match for their wards, besides religion and caste, region also plays an important role. For cultural differences they are not prepared to marry their wards to other Indian communities like Punjabis, Marwaris and Sindhis. As they want to find a spouse for their wards from the same caste and region, very often they look to India to find such a match. It has already been said that many Gorakhpuris have not brought their families to Bangkok. Even those who live with their families, send their marriageable daughters to India to live with their cousins or with other relatives. In the process they protect their daughters from too much exposure to an alien culture and also get help from their cousins to find a suitable match. Generally, the marriages of Gorakhpuris are held in India. Very few marriages have taken place in Thailand. There are many Gorakhpuris who cannot afford to visit India to attend the marriages of their wards. Such people compensate for their absence by sending enough money. Before settling a marriage, all Gorakhpuris match the horoscope of the boy and the girl. The date and time of marriage is also fixed in consultation with a priest.

There are few cases of marriages between Indian males and Thai girls. Majority of such marriages have taken place among third generation of migrants. No one in the first generation married Thai but there were few marriages between second generation males and Thai girls. All such marriages have taken place between Indian males and Thai girls. No Indian girl has married Thai boy. This suggests that Indians are ready to accept Thai girls as daughter-in-law but do not want to marry their daughter to Thai boys (Hussain, 1982).

Language

For survival in Thailand learning of Thai language is a necessity. All Punjabis both Hindus and Sikhs who became citizen of Thailand had acquired proficiency not only in speaking but also in reading and writing of Thai language. In fact majority of the Punjabi families are bilingual. Old members of the families prefer to speak Punjabi whereas younger generation give preference to Thai. Though younger people prefer Thai, yet they are also taught Punjabi and sometime special classes are held in Gurdwara for this purpose. This is applicable to both boys and girls. Though Punjabis had learned Thai, a necessity to run the business but still had not given up their mother tongue. Some of the young people use Thai even while communicating with their parents at home. Hindi and English are the other languages in which majority of the Punjabis can communicate besides Punjabi and Thai (Mishra, 2004).

Traditional dialect of Bhojpuri is commonly used by Gorakhpuris while talking among themselves. Hindi is used while talking to other Indians. All of them have acquired a working knowledge of Thai which is essential to carry out their economic activities. While interacting with local people Thai is used.

Food

Preference for Indian food is weakness of all immigrants from India irrespective of the country of their migration. The immigrants in Thailand are no exception. At home only Indian food of *dal* (split bean), vegetables and chapatti is served. There are few persons both young and old who have developed taste for Thai dishes—both vegetarian and non-vegetatian. To cater the need of individuals who are living alone in Thailand there are number of Indian restaurants where Indian food is available. Majority of Punjabis in Thailand prefer to eat normal Indian food of *dal* (split beans), vegetables, chapatti, and rice. Once in a while Thai food may be cooked at home as the younger generation have developed a taste for Thai food—both vegetarian and non-vegetarian.

Gorakhpuris generally prefer to eat Indian dishes only. There are a few Gorakhpuris, especially the Brahmans whose families live in India, cook their own food at home. They cannot tolerate the smell of Thai food and secondly they don't want to eat food cooked by somebody else for purity and pollution. Since most of them are vegetarians, they are not sure of getting pure vegetarian food in a restaurant.

There are many restaurants in Bangkok where Indian food is available. In Phaurat area only, there were 16 restaurants in 1989 owned by Indians , four by Nepalis and two by Bangladeshis where Indian food was available. Nepali restaurants were mainly used by those people who were living alone as they were cooking Indian food and their charges were less as compared to other places. One Thai woman, who worked as a maid with an Indian family also opened a small outfit to offer Indian food. Another place where Indian dishes are available is the third floor of ATM departmental store in Phaurat market. There are many stalls offering varieties of Indian delicacies which are managed by Nepali and Punjabi women. There are number of other Indian restaurants all over Bangkok where all varieties of Indian delicacies are available. This indicates that those Punjabis who did not like Thai food and are living alone in Thailand there is no dearth of Indian food (Gupta, 1999).

Cultural Diacritical

Majority of the Sikhs in Thailand have kept their five K's (*Panj Kakka*) intact which is a part of their traditional dress. The five K's are *kesh* uncut hair, *kanga* (comb), *kirpan* (small dagger), *kara* (steel wrist bangle) and *kaccha* (a pair of breeches which must not reach below the knee). *Kara*, *kesh* and *kirpan* are visible diacritical marks and majority of the Sikhs in Thailand possess them. Turban is a symbol of Sikhism and most of the Sikhs wear it. There are few Sikhs specially among younger generation who are keeping beard but not long hair but while visiting Gurdwara they use turban. Very few Sikhs carry kirpan all the time.

Women had not discarded their traditional dress of *salwar* (loose trousers) and *kameez* (tunic covering the upper part of a woman's body) and *sari* but young girls had adopted jeans and other Western style dresses as used by Thai women. Almost all Sikh women, young and old wear *kara* on their right wrist. The status of women had not changed except that now they are helping their menfolk in business activities. Some young girls have started working as sales girls, secretaries and teachers. Since Hindu Punjabis and Sikhs both belong to the same cultural region, there are many similarities in their style of living and the dressing pattern. The majority of the Hindu Punjabi women wear their traditional dress of sari and *salwar kameez*, though some women, young and middle-aged, have started wearing jeans. They put bangles on their arms—the more prosperous wear gold bangles but a large majority of them wear glass bangles and also apply a *bindi* on their forehead. A few Punjabi women sprinkle vermilion on their hair parting. Like Sikh women, the status of Hindu Punjabi women has also changed. Though household chores continue to be their main activity, some young girls and middle-aged women have started participating in social, cultural and economic activities.

Living in Thailand has not affected the lifestyle and dressing pattern of the Gorakhpuris and as such they are easily identifiable. Both males and females wear their traditional dresses. Generally, Gorakhpuri males still wear *dhoti-kurta* or *payjama-kurta*; some may be found wearing bushshirt and pants. Male

Brahamans use a tilak on their forehead, a traditional diacritical mark for the priestly group. Gorakhpuri females wear traditional dress of sari. They also wear glass bangles and apply a *bindi* on their forehead and sprinkle vermilion on their hair parting, a mark of their marital bliss. Gorakhpuri women do not go out for work. Almost all of them remain confined to the home. Many of these women cover their heads (half veiling their faces) when they walk with their spouses in the city.

Change of Names

It is mandatory for all migrants who have become Thai citizen to have a Thai name. Indians who have taken Thai citizenship generally print their original name as well as Thai name on their visiting cards. But most of the time they are called by their Indian names.

Contacts with India and Parent Culture

All Indian families maintain their links with India in one way or the other. Some visit India regularly either to renew contacts with their consanguineal and affinal relations, or to find a suitable match for their children. Those who have migrated with the entire family and do not have any near relations in India, visit the country either for sightseeing or to pay visit to religious places. Those families whose children are studying in India, sometimes escort their children to school. Discussions with various persons revealed that their family members visit India more frequently. First generation migrants visited India more frequently. Among third generation very few have visited India (Hussain, 1982).

Indian films and music are quite popular among all Punjabi families. Most of the families watch Indian films in the comforts of their homes as Video is possessed by almost all families. Now DVD have replaced Video. The cassettes and CD of films including those which have not yet been released in India are available in most of the shops in Phaurat market. Some enterprising Punjabis have started home deliveries of CD and cassettes. Besides film songs, some of the Ghazal singers like Pankaj Udas, Anoop Jalota, Chitra and Jagjit Singh are also quite popular.

Gorakhpuris like to watch Hindi films and listen to Indian film songs. Those who cannot afford to buy a VCR or VCP, visit their friends to see the films or see them at public places like ATM departmental store. On the top floor of ATM departmental store in the Phaurat market where all Indian delicacies are available, a restaurant has also been opened. This restaurant not only provides Indian food cooked by Nepali girls but also shows Indian films or song sequences from Indian films throughout the day. Many Gorakhpuris regularly visit this restaurant and sit there for hours together and watch these films.

Schooling of Children

For the benefit of the children of Indians in Bangkok, Hindu Samaj and Sri Guru Singh Sabha run their schools. This is one of the various public welfare activities undertaken by the associations of Hindus and Sikhs. Bhartiya Vidyalaya, the school managed by the Hindu Samaj was started in 1934. All the teachers employed were Indians and in the beginning only the children of Indians were admitted. At that time even Urdu was also taught in the school. It was done as majority of the Punjabi migrants were familiar with this language. It was also a part of curriculum in the schools of Punjab at that time. The school was a part of the temple compiex. Till 1962, it was only a primary school with classes upto seventh standard. It was upgraded to the tenth class in 1962. With the expansion of the school, Thai children are also admitted. More than eighty per cent of the children studying in this school are local Thais and the rest are Indians.

Only one foreign language can be taught in a school according to Thai law. Since English is taught as a foreign language, special arrangements are made to teach Hindi to Indian students. Special classes are held after the regular school hours to teach Hindi. The students from the first standard to the fourth standard are grouped together; and the students of fifth to eighth standard form another group. The Hindi teaching course was registered with Rashtra Bhasha Prachar Samiti in Wardha (Maharashtra) in 1967, and the syllabus evolved by the

Rashtra Bhasha Prachar Samiti, Wardha is followed. Hindi classes are held twice a week, each for an hour's duration.

The school observes all the holidays declared by the Thai government besides closing for some Indian festivals like Diwali, Dussehra and Krishna Janmashtmi. The school also observes Independence Day of India (15 August), Republic Day (26 January), the birthday of Mahatma Gandhi (2 October) and the birthday of Jawaharlal Nehru (14 November). There is an elected board to look after the day-to-day management and running of the institute.

The school is a good example of racial affinity between the Thais and the Indians, and this feeling is sprouted and nourished by the environment as well as the curricula of the school. Since both the languages—Thai as well as Hindi—are taught, the Indian children speak Thai fluently. Similarly, some Hindi words have entered the vocabulary of the Thai students. Children who attend this school generally belong to a lower socio-economic status. Among Indians, some Gorakhpuris and a few Punjabis both the Sikhs and non-Sikhs send their children to this school. The majority of the Gorakhpuris prefer to send their children to India for schooling. Hindu Punjabis either send their children to international schools in Bangkok or to India. Very often Punjabi children come to India for study after completing their primary education in Bangkok.

The school managed by Sri Guru Singh Sabha, called Sikh Vidyalaya is one of the most important activities of the association. Though the school started in 1951, it was in 1985 that it was expanded. Currently, the school has two sections: (i) Primary section, and (ii) High School section. The High School section has two divisions, i.e. English division and the Thai division. Although the buildings of both these schools are adjacent to each other, they have a separate management. The Thai medium school is managed by the Thai staff; the students are also local Thais. The High School sections are run in two separate building in Bangna, some 30 kilometres away.

In 1951, the school was run in a five-storey building adjacent to the Gurdwara in Phaurat market. The syllabus of the Education Ministry of the Royal Thai Government was adopted. The level of education provided to the students was up to M.S.3 (equivalent to matriculation of the Punjab University). Admission was open to all irrespective of race or nationality. Free education was given to the needy and deserving candidates. Financial aid was also provided by the Thai government. Out of 33 teachers only five of them were Indians including the Principal.

Prior to 1985 some of the affluent parents sent their children (both boys and girls) to India, especially to Mussoorie and Delhi, for education. But after the 1984 riots against the Sikhs (when one Sikh bodyguard of the late Prime Minister Indira Gandhi shot her dead) the executive committee of Shri Guru Singh Sabha took a decision to start their own English medium school in Bangkok. The land was purchased on the outskirts of Bangkok about 30 kilometres from Phaurat. The Principal of the Guru Nanak Mission School Mussoorie, where the older generation went for studies, was invited by the Singh Sabha to head the English section as the Director. The school started functioning in March 1985 with 164 students. Most of these students got themselves transferred from Mussoorie. The school runs classes from fourth to tenth. The Sikh Vidyalaya in Bangna is spread over more than five acres of land. The school provides facilities for some outdoor games like hockey, cricket, badminton, football, volleyball, basket ball and tennis. The school is planning to have its own swimming pool and also a hostel. Right now, it is only a day school. The school was shifted to the present site only in August 1986. There were fifteen teachers including two British. The rest of the teachers were Indians. In 1989, the building had four storeys. On the ground floor is the director's room and one big hall with a stage. At the back of the stage, the holy book of Sikhs (*Granth Sahib*) is displayed on a decorated platform. On occasions the hall is used for religious purposes. Generally, this hall is used when dignitaries are invited to speak to students. On week days it is used as music class. The music lessons are given in playing instruments such as the tabla. Children are also taught to sing, particularly, Gurbani (the recital of poems from Sikh religious books).

Students at this school come from different communities including the Hindus and Muslims. Students from countries other than India such as Bangladesh, Hong Kong, Singapore and Malaysia also study in the school. The students are divided into four "houses" named after the four sons of Guru Gobind Singh: Ajit house, Juhar house, Zorawar house and Fateh house. The school organizes inter-house competitions in games and elocution. During the annual function, students participate in Hindi, Punjabi, or English plays, sing geedha and also participate in bhangra (a major folk dance of Punjab). Geedha and bhangra are the most popular programmes.

The school is affiliated to the University of London and the students are offered a General Certificate of Education. Among the various courses, Hindi and Punjabi are also taught. The teaching of Punjabi was introduced in 1988 on a special request from some of the parents. In 1988, 15 students appeared for the Punjabi examination and 7 for Hindi. Most of the students resist learning of these languages as they consider Thai as their mother tongue.

The Primary section of the Sikh Vidyalaya is located on the top floor of Gurdwara in Phaurat area. The learning of Thai language is compulsory for all the students. The students can learn either Hindi or Punjabi as their second language. The school offers training in Indian classical music at the nursery level. They also learn singing of Gurbani. The school has Indian as well as Thai teachers. The school has an air conditioned van to transport students from home to school and back. The school admits children of all religions. This school prepares students for the English medium school in Bangna. The students are served Indian food, but Thai noodles are also served.

Some Sikhs prefer to send their children to international schools in Bangkok, while a few parents send their children to Thai schools. There are three International schools in Bangkok, i.e. International School of Bangkok, Ruamrudee International School and Bangkok Pattana. Since the tuition fee in the Sikh Vidyalaya and International School is very high it is beyond the reach of a large number of Sikhs. Such parents and those who do not want to send their children to Thai schools beyond primary education, send their children to India for studies. They find education in India less costly than Bangkok. This also exposes them to Indian culture.

Associations

To keep the parent culture alive and to transmit the cultural values to younger generation all Indian communities form their associations. All religious and cultural activities of the communities are organized through these associations. In Thailand also various Indian communities have formed their association. In this section the associations of Sikhs and Hindus have been discussed.

All activities of Sikhs in Bangkok are organized by Sri Guru Singh Sabha, the central organization of Sikhs in Thailand. This is a registered body and recognized by the Thai Government. The affairs of the Sabha are looked after by a management committee which consists of 15 members who are elected for two years. Any person who is 25 years of age and able to read and write Punjabi is eligible to become member of the committee. The clean shaven are not eligible for the membership of the committee. No person can remain a member of the committee for more than two terms. Sub-committees are formed to look after the Gurdwara and various other activities such as school, medical centre, library, old age home, orphanage, ladies and youth organizations.

All Hindu communities have their own associations such as the Marwari association, Sindhi association and Gujarati association. But only two associations, one of Gorakhpuris and the other of Punjabi Hindus are more prominent and well-known. The association of Gorakhpuris is known as Hindu Dharma Sabha and that of Punjabis is called Hindu Samaj.

The Hindu Dharma Sabha is an old association formed by the Hindus on 18 April 1915. This is a registered association and its office is located in the premises of Vishnu Mandir at 50 Thung Wat Don Tanuawa in Bangkok. The membership of this Sabha is open to all Hindus who are residents of Thailand and are above 18 years of age. Those who have faith in Hindu philosophy, but are not Hindus by birth can also become its members. There are two kinds of membership: (i) Life membership and (ii) Ordinary membership. The Management Committee consists of 21 members and its life is only for one year.

This association of Hindu Punjabis came into existence around 1927-28. The management committee consists of 12 members, who are elected every year. This is a registered association. The constitution of the committee clearly indicates the activities undertaken by the Hindu Samaj. Women members of the Hindu Samaj have started a separate organization called Mahila Satsang. It was started about 25 years ago and in the beginning they used to meet at the homes of different members. But since 1982, they have started organising the Satsang in the temple premises. They meet every Tuesday. No other Satsang can be fixed on this day. The birthdays of their grandchildren are also celebrated in the Satsang. Besides contributing to the Hindu Samaj, they also contribute funds for lunch. The lunch is cooked by Punjabi ladies hired by them.

Religious Activities

Temples and festivals are important part of Indian migrants. Irrespective of the country of their settlement they construct their religious places of worship and celebrate various festivals and other cultural programmes. In this section, the activities of religious places of Hindus and Sikhs have been discussed.

(a) Sri Guru Singh Sabha Gurdwara

By 1911, a large number of Sikh families, both Keshdhari and Sahajdhari had settled in Thailand, mostly in Bangkok. At that time, there was no formal Sikh temple in Bangkok. On every Sunday, on every full moon day, as well as on the birth anniversaries of various Gurus (called Guruparva) these people used to gather in the houses of Sikhs by rotation and hold their religious congregations. In 1912, the local Sikh community decided to construct a Gurdwara in Bangkok. Accordingly, a house was rented out near the Phaurat intersection. Later on a wooden house was taken on lease in 1913 on a long-term basis in the Italian lane on Phaurat road to install Guru Granth Sahib (Holy Book) and to hold prayers. There was provision for free meals and free lodging for the sojourners. The teaching of Punjabi was also introduced in Bangkok in the same year. From 1913 to 1932 the Sikh Sangat (congregation) of Thailand organized its meetings here to support the freedom movement in India by indirect participation and through financial support to freedom fighters.

With the increase in number of Sikh families need was felt to construct a Gurdwara on their own land. A piece of land on the southwest of the then Gurdwara was purchased in 1932. A plan was prepared to construct a three-storeyed building. Nine representatives were given responsibility to raise funds. This Gurdwara was declared open to the public in 1933 and langar (free community meal) was served to all at the end of Sri Akhand Path (a continuous reading of Guru Granth Sahib for forty-eight hours). The building was illuminated at night. A trust of five members from the nine representatives was formed to manage the Gurdwara affairs. It also started a Khalsa School where Punjabi, Urdu and English were taught. Later on a few more members were added to the trust for the efficient functioning of the Gurdwara activities.

During the Second World War, Netaji Subhash Chandra Bose, the famous freedom fighter came to Thailand in his bid to reorganize his Azad Hind Fauz (Indian National Army) for the liberation of India. All Indians, including Sikhs, volunteered themselves to join the army. They gave their whole-heart financial and moral support to Netaji for the reorganization of the Indian Independence League. Sardar Ishar Singh Narula, one of the trustees of the Gurdwara was elected Chairman of the Bangkok Branch of INA. During the Second World War, Bangkok was heavily bombarded by the allied air forces. In one bombing the allied forces targeted the memorial bridge and the metropolitan powerhouse, both quite adjacent to the Gurdwara. The bombs went off the target and fell on the top terrace of the Gurdwara building and pierced through to the second floor but remained unexploded. At that time several hundred persons were taking shelter on the ground floor of the shrine and all of them had a miraculous escape, for which they thanked the Guru Granth Sahib.

More Sikh families migrated to Bangkok after partition of India in 1947 and thus the population of Sikhs in Bangkok increased considerably. The increase in the influx of Sikhs into Thailand compelled the management committee to undertake the remodeling of the Gurdwara. The present Gurdwara is a result of that remodeling. The present Gurdwara is a six-storeyed building. On the ground floor, apart from the office of the Gurdwara Committee, there is a storeroom, free dispensary and a kitchen for cooking langar on religious and other functions. On the first floor, are living quarters for its employees. The library is also on the same floor. There are also some rooms for sojourners. On the third floor, is a big dining hall for community meals. The hall on the fourth floor is used for social functions. There is a spacious assembly hall on the fifth floor, where the sangat gathers daily to listen to recitals from the Holy Granth Sahib. A specially erected place has been provided in the hall from where the Sikh preacher gives his sermons. The hall is completely carpeted. On the sixth floor a primary school is run by the Gurudwara Committee. The entire building is centrally air conditioned and also fitted with two elevators.

The programmes for the whole month including the announcement of langar are displayed on the ground floor. A separate place has been reserved on the ground floor where devotees remove their shoes. Since the Sikh religion does not allow devotees to enter the main hall bare headed, a white handkerchief is kept on a small stool just outside the assembly hall for those who do not wear turban. Ladies cover their heads with a dupatta or sari before entering the main hall. A worshipper approaches the dais upon which the Guru Granth Sahib rests, there he/she bows and makes an offering of cash. Careful not to turn his or her back on the book, the worshipper then sits with the congregation on the carpet. As a convention and custom, men sit on the left hand side and women on the right hand side, but they sit separately. Service in the Gurdwara is generally held in the morning for one hour. On Sundays, it lasts for an hour and a half when the congregation is much larger. Most of the Punjabi businessmen of the Phaurat market begin their day by visiting the Gurdwara. Punjabi is used in all the activities of the Gurdwara. However, the pamphlets and booklets are published either in both the languages or in Thai or in Punjabi. The document to be submitted to the Thai Government is published either in Thai and in English.

Hindu Temples

There are five Hindu temples in Bangkok. They are: (i) Sri Maha Mariamman temple; (ii) Hindu Dharma Sabha Mandir, (iii) Dev Mandir; (iv) Ram Nayan temple and (v) Lord Vishnu temple. The description of each of these temples is in order:

(a) Sri Maha Mariamman temple

This is the oldest among the Hindu temples in Bangkok. It is said that in 1870, the Tamil community of Bangkok, who started migrating to Siam and adjoining areas during the reigns of Sri Vijay and Dvaravati purchased a plot of land (the present site of the temple on Silom Road) for building the temple with the help and assistance of the local people. Before that they had installed an idol of the Hindu goddess Sri Maha Mariamman in a small house under a tree behind the sugar plantation near the windmill road, now known as Silom Road. The migration of Tamils paved the way for the rapid spread of the Dravidian ancient culture and civilization in Siam. The influence of Hindu culture, customs and tradition found their way into the fabric of the social life of the people of Siam. It is said that the ancient and the most holy Brahmanic Vedic Book of Thailand was written in the ancient Tamil script and this is still available in the Thai Brahman temple in Bangkok.

Since the Tamilians had married the natives, the culture of these people found easy acceptance among the natives. Besides incorporating a multitude of words from Tamil, Pali and Sanskrit into the Thai society, the locals also became devotees of Goddess Mariamman. Thus, the shrine of Goddess Mariamman became a place of worship for all including Thais. In 1872, King Chulalongkorn of Thailand came to India and on his return he gifted a set of glass lamps to the temple as a token of friendship between India and Thailand.

By the joint efforts of the Tamil community and others the temple was renovated and a boundary wall was constructed in 1911. Gradually, idols of Hindu gods and goddesses were brought from India and installed with due solemnity and reverence in the temple. Idols included Lord Ganesh, Lord Subramanium, Lord Krishna and Sri Maha Mariamman. All the important festivals of Hindus are celebrated here. In 1915, a new committee was formed and officially registered with the government authorities as *The Temple Trustee–Sri Mahariamman alias Sri Maha Umadevi*. The celebrations of annual Navaratri and the Vijay Dasmi (Dushera) festival were suspended during the Second World War, when the conditions were not favourable. However, the celebrations were revived with the return of normalcy. In 1953, a huge image of Lord Buddha was consecrated in the temple premises with a view to making it a place of worship for the Hindus and the Buddhists alike. The temple was further renovated with the help of the temple architects from India in 1970. The management of the temple is looked after by a committee consisting of five members and a few advisors.

All the important Hindu and Buddhist ceremonies are organized here. The temple has Tamil priests who have completely assimilated into Thai culture. They have married the local Thais and speak the Thai language. In fact, nowadays, this temple is visited more by local Thais than any other community.

(b) Hindu Dharma Sabha Mandir

This temple is commonly called Vishnu temple. It is located at 50 Donkusol Yannawa Bangkok which is about 10 kms. from Phaurat market. In 1915, five prominent persons (Shri Lala Sundar Das Punjabi, Shri Uma Shanker Chaubey, Shri Ram Dev Ojha and two more) decided to open a Hindu temple in Bangkok. Before the constructed of this temple Hindus used to visit Maha Mariamman temple for worship. This temple was ready in 1920. Since then the location of the temple has remained the same but a few modifications have been made like the addition of the outside main hall, guesthouse and a library. The building is a single storey. The outside main hall was constructed in 1971, whereas the foundation stone for the guest house and the library was laid in 1974. People contributed liberally for the construction of the guesthouse and library. At one stage all the Hindus used to visit this temple, but after the construction of the Dev Samaj Mandir, the Punjabi Hindus have stopped visiting this temple because of the distance. The main idol in this temple is that of Lord Krishna. There are also idols of other goddesses.

The library is located in a big hall which contains the portraits of the former and the present Prime Ministers and the Presidents of India. The portraits of Fakruddin Ali Ahmed, Neelam Sanjiva Reddy, Giani Zail Singh, Pandit Jawaharlal Nehru, Indira Gandhi, Lal Bahadur Shastri and Rajiv Gandhi are there. The portraits of the King of Thailand and that of Mahatma Gandhi are also there. The library opens only on Sundays. Most of the books in the library are in Hindi. In the backyard of the temple there are six rooms which have been rented to six families. All of them are from Gorakhpuris.

(c) Dev Samaj Mandir

This is the third Hindu temple built by Indians currently living in Bangkok. The process was initiated by a group of Punjabis in 1927-28. In the beginning the Dev Samaj Mandir was located in the Phaurat market in a two-storeyed building hired on rent. At that time a small school for Indian children was run in the second storey and the Mandir was on the ground floor. In 1940, the land was purchased and the mandir was shifted to the present location in a two-storeyed building which is about a 10-minute walk from the Phaurat market. Bharat Vidyalaya (Indian school) is run on the ground floor and the Mandir is on the first floor. The second storey to the building was added in 1969 and the Mandir was shifted to this storey. The first floor hall is converted into a dining hall.

Before 1940, the Association which constructed the building was called Hindu Sabha but in 1940 its name was changed to Hindu Samaj. This was done so that Hindus of different sects, including the Arya Samaj, could also become its members. The executive committee of the temple consisted of all Hindu Punjabis. In this temple, the idols and images of all the Hindu gods can be seen.

(d) Ram Nayan Mandir

This is a small temple as compared to the other three temples. The temple is located in the Petchburi area of Thonburi, about two kilometres from Phaurat. The temple is named after the person who was responsible for its construction. The temple is located in a small single-storey house and was built in 1969-70. Mr. Ram Nayan died few years ago at the age of 103 years. He came to Bangkok at the age of 50. Before coming to Bangkok, he was in Burma (now Myanmar) where he was leading the life of a dacoit. In Burma he had a gang of about 100 persons. As the Burmese government took strict measures to control his activities, he migrated to Bangkok and changed his lifestyle. He was responsible for the construction of this temple. This temple is more often visited by ladies, both the Punjabis and Gorakhpuris, living in Thonburi. Monday is the special day when one can see a large number of ladies at the temple. These women come to offer their prayers to Shiva Lingam, which is kept on a wooden platform in an open space. They generally come in a group of five to six.

There is no committee to look after the temple activities. Mr. Ram Nayan while dying donated this property to a certain Mrs. Pushpawati who is generally called Mataji. Right now everything related to this temple is managed by her. No repair work has been done for many years for the lack of funds. Somebody now has donated 50,000 Baht for the renovation of the building.

(e) Lord Vishnu Temple

The India-Thai Chamber of Commerce in Bangkok presented an idol of Lord Vishnu on February 26, 1984 to the Governor of the Bangkok Metropolitan Administration who received the idol on behalf of the Prime Minister of Thailand. The idol has been installed in an open space in the park in front of the Dev Samaj temple and the place is very near the Giant Swing and the Thai Hindu temple. It was presented in commemoration of Rattanakosin (Bangkok) Bicentennial year, celebrated in 1982. A donation of 7,38,100 Baht was collected for this purpose. Twelve business firms gave a donation of 25 thousand Baht each, another 12 firms gave 15 thousand Baht each and 34 firms donated less than 15 thousand Baht each. In all, 58 business firms donated the money. It is important to mention that all the Indian communities of Bangkok including the Sikhs and Muslims gave donations. In fact, at that time a Namdhari Sikh was the President of the India-Thai Chambers of Commerce. There are two priests to look after this temple and both of them are Gorakhpuris.

Festivals

There are three festivals which have found a prominent place among Sikhs in Bangkok. Baisakhi and Diwali were included by Guru Amar Das (1552-74), while Holi was added by Guru Gobind Singh (1675-1708). These three festivals along with various Guruparvas (including the birth anniversaries of various Gurus) are celebrated by the Sikhs in Bangkok. Among various anniversaries, the birthdays of Guru Nanak and Guru Gobind Singh and the Martyrdom day of the fifth Guru Arjun are the most important.

Baisakhi is generally celebrated by the Punjabis on 13 April every year as New Year's Day. "The date is fixed, being based on a solar calendar, once every thirty-six years it occurs on 14 April" (Cole and Sambhi, 1978: 129). This is also the day, the Thais celebrate the Songkran festival. While Baisakhi is observed among both the Sikhs and the Punjabi Hindus, the way of its celebration differs in them. On this day Hindus offer barley and grain to the Brahmans from the crops to be harvested, whereas the Sikhs pay homage to their Gurus and listen to their teaching. On Baisakhi day in 1699, Guru Gobind Singh formed the Khalsa brotherhood. It was on this day that in 1919 General Dyer tried to prevent the Sikh assembly in Jallianwala Bagh in Amritsar (India) when three hundred and thirty-seven men and forty-one children were shot dead by the British Army on General Dyer's order (c.f. *Ibid.* 130).

All the religious festivals of Hindus are celebrated by the Indian Community in Bangkok. One important aspect is that most of the festivals are celebrated jointly in temples. The most important festivals celebrated by Hindus in Bangkok are Shivratri,

Holi, Navratri, Dussehra and Diwali. Some of the festivals like Shivratri, Navratri are celebrated in Dev Samaj Mandir in which all the Hindus living in Bangkok participate, whereas Holi is mainly celebrated by Gorakhpuri in Vishnu temple.

On the occasion of the sixtieth birthday of H.M., the King of Thailand, Bhumbol Adulyadej in 1987, "sacred water" was collected from all the religious places from every district of Thailand for final presentation to the king by the Chief Brahman Priest of Thailand. To show their gratitude and pay homage to the king, various Hindu associations of Bangkok decided to mix Ganges water from India, as a part of "sacred water" for the religious ceremony to be performed for the king. The Ganges water was presented to the Chief Brahman Priest at Wat Suthat with great fanfare on 29 November 1987.

The summing up of the adoption process of Indians in Thailand on various indicators of sandwich culture has been presented in this section:

I. **Apertures**

(i) Intermarriages (breakdown of endogamy)

- Majority of the marriages among Gorakhpuris in Bangkok are endogamous. Their first choice is to select a mate for their wards from India who may belong to same religion and caste.
- Hindu Punjabis are accepting Thai girls as their daughters-in-law. But such cases are not many and most of such cases belong to younger generation of migrants. Preference is given to the person of same caste who may be from India, or some body from Thailand itself.
- By and large Sikhs prefer to marry their ward in Sikh families only who may belong to same caste. Like Hindu Punjabis they are accepting Thai girls as daughters-in-law. They have widen their scope to Sikhs settled in neighbouring countries such as Singapore, Malaysia and Hong Kong.
- Marriages between Indian girls and Thai boys have not been found. This means that Indians are not ready to marry their girls to Thai boys.

(ii) Adoption of names of the host society

It is mandatory for those foreigners who have taken Thai citizenship to have Thai name. All Indians who have become citizen of Thailand, write Thai as well as Indian names on their visiting cards. However, very often they are addressed by their Indian names. They all like to be called by their Indian name.

(iii) Adoption of the language

Adoption of Thai language is a necessity for survival. All migrants have to learn the language at least pick some Thai words. This is more so for those who are in business. Old migrants among Indians have learnt the language, but the younger generation of Punjabis, both Hindus and Sikhs not only speak but also can read and write. Very few among Gorakhpuris can write but quite a few can read. But older generation among Gorakhpuris can speak fluently.

(iv) Religious conversion

Official religion of Thailand is Buddhism which is an offshoot of Hinduism and has borrowed many elements from it. Despite many similarities between two religions no case of conversion to Buddhism has been found among Indians. Very often one can find local people visiting Hindu temples and offering prayers.

(v) Adoption of the food habits and developing taste for host society cuisine

- Younger generation of Punjabis, both Hindus and Sikhs have developed taste for Thai dishes. In school and outside they prefer to eat Thai food. However, at home they have to consume Indian food as most the older generation stick to their traditional food. Very few among Gorakhpuris have developed taste for Thai food. Some of them cook their own food as they do not like the smell of Thai food.

II. Insulatory Mechanisms

(i) Retention of mother tongue

Indians not only prefer to use their mother tongue in day-to-day conversation but also make attempt to teach to the younger generation. Besides using it at home and at religious places special arrangements are made to teach mother tongue to the younger generation. They also learn the mother tongue by watching Indian movies and listening to Indian songs.

(ii) Separate educational facilities

Hindu Punjabi and Sikhs in Thailand have opened their own schools. Though local children are also admitted to these schools, yet special arrangements are made to familiarize Indian children to their parent culture.

(iii) Concentration of living quarters

The areas of concentration of Hindu Punjabis and Sikhs are different than the Gorakhpuris. Hindu Punjabis and Sikhs have their concentration in some posh colonies like Sukhumvit. Majority of Gorakhpuris either living in Thonburi or around Vishnu temple and both these areas are not inhabited by middle-class people.

(iv) Endogamy

By and large Indians in Thailand have maintained their endogamous status. There are few cases where Hindu Punjabis and Sikhs have accepted Thai girls as daughter-in-law but no Indian girl has married Thai boy.

(v) Voluntary organizations

All Indians in Thailand have formed their associations. Various religious and cultural functions are organized through these associations which keep the parent culture alive.

(vi) Parental religion

No case of religious conversion has been found in Thailand. All Indians have freedom to pursue their religious activities in Thailand.

(vii) Concentration in certain occupations

Majority of the Indians in Thailand are businessmen. Most of them are in textile business. Only Pandits from Gorakhpur are engaged in their traditional activities. Their services are hired by all Hindu Punjabis and Gorakhpuris.

(viii) Continuation of food habits and taboos

Except younger generation of Hindu Punjabis and Sikhs who have developed taste for Thai food, all other migrants from India prefer to have Indian food. Majority of the Gorakhpuris observe all the taboos and prefer to cook their own food.

(ix) Cultural diacriticals

Sikhs in Thailand have maintained their physical diacritical marks. All of them wear turban and keep beard and also wear kara on their wrist. Even those who have cut their hair short wear turban. Majority of the Gorakhpuri males wear their traditional dress of kurta and dhoti. Pandits use tilak on their forehead. Except younger generation of females among Hindu Punjabis and Sikhs who have started using western dress of jeans and skirt, all other women wear saree or salwar kameez. All Gorakhpuri ladies wear sarees.

(x) Contact with parent culture

All Indians including Hindu Punjabis and Sikhs remain in constant touch with their friends and relatives in India. The families of some of the Gorakhpuri migrants visit them during summer vacations. Some of them also approach their relatives to find suitable match for their wards. Another way to remain in touch with the parent culture is through newspaper and films.

Summing Up

Variations in the adaptation process of Thai culture in three Indian communities may be attributed to differences in cultural, contextual and situational factors. Hindu Punjabis and Sikhs hail from the same region, i.e. Punjab and the cultural background of both these communities is more or less the same. Their level of acculturation in Thailand is also similar. They have created more apertures and are open to new influences. A distinctive feature of Punjabi culture is their adaptability and openness to change. This is due to the fact that most alien cultures came to India from the North-West and Punjab being geographically closest to the border had the maximum impact. Thus, Punjab became a melting pot of various composite cultures, indigenous and foreign, which gradually were incorporated in what came to be known as Punjabi culture. "This cultural co-mingling between people of different regions, with different social systems, gave birth to a culture with a liberal outlook" (Dalip Singh, 1981: 3). Immigrants with this kind of cultural background would certainly be more adaptable in a different society. Since both Hindu Punjabis and Sikhs migrated to Thailand with their families, it established the fact that these people went with the intention of settling there permanently. This intention has perhaps played a crucial role in their positive attitude towards the adaptation process. One of the best indicators of their receptive approach is that they have started accepting Thai girls as their daughters-in-law. Though the number of such cases is small, the first dent has certainly been made.

As compared to Hindu Punjabis and Sikhs, Gorakhpuris are more rigid and traditional. They hail from a region in India which is insulated and has not been exposed to other cultures. In Thailand they have isolated themselves and "shy away" not only from local Thais but from other Indian groups also. They have accepted only the language of the Thais, since it was necessary for their existence in Thailand. The majority of them went to Thailand not to settle permanently but to make their fortune or at least eke out a living. This has influenced their attitude towards the Thais. A large number of them migrated alone and never carried their families along. Old members went back and were replaced by younger ones. The majority have their primary and secondary relatives in India and close links are maintained with them. They have kept themselves aloof and did not make any attempt to assimilate in Thai society. They are also very critical of the social structure of the host society. For instance, they are very critical of the freedom and emancipation of Thai women. Such an attitude creates psychological barriers and does not allow them to make any attempt for assimilation in the host society.

The presence of more insulatory mechanisms among Gorakhpuris makes them less vulnerable to assimilation. Gorakhpuris are happy to be "sojourners" who live as aliens in an alien society always maintaining their "separateness" and mingling only with the host society where it is absolutely necessary. After they have saved enough or are tired and old they go back to India and may be replaced by another batch of immigrants.

CHAPTER-5

Emerging Sandwich Cultures: A Comparative Perspective

Cultural conditions of the Indians settled abroad varied substantially and so their contextual and situational conditions which had bearing on their adaptation and adjustment at the place of settlement. Majority of the Indians in various countries have been sandwiched between the parent culture and the culture of the host society, but the nature and degree of sandwich culture differs from group to group and from country to country. Some of them, without compromising their own values and beliefs accepted the cultural traits of the host society, whereas there were others who accepted only those cultural traits, which were necessary for their survival. It has been observed by many scholars that majority of the Indians prefer cultural preservation with economic integration. Depending upon their cultural, contextual and situational conditions, the cultural preservation, however, may vary from group to group and people to people. In the process, majority of the immigrants are sandwiched between the two cultures. Some immigrants may open more apertures to mingle in the host society, but there might be others who may prefer to insulate themselves from the host culture to preserve their cultural identity. In this study, the impact of cultural, contextual and situational conditions on the adaptation process of Indians settled in three countries, namely Trinidad, United States of America, and Thailand have been examined. Each of these countries provided different contextual and situational conditions and even the cultural conditions of migrants from India differed significantly, which substantially influenced their adaptation and adjustment process. An examination of all these processes will be useful in determining the degree and the extent to which these people have been able to open apetures or insulat themselves to be sandwiched between the parent culture and the host culture. As mentioned earlier the data have been culled from the available studies of these countries. A comparative perspective of Indian immigrants in different countries has been discussed in this chapter. First we will examine the impact of these conditions separately for each country and then the comparative picture has been presented.

Depending upon the cultural conditions and destination Indian immigrants considered in this study have been classified in the following categories:

1. Indians who migrated as indentured labour.
2. Indians who migrated on their own and also decided their own destination. These can further be classified into following sub-categories.
   (a) Those early immigrants who went to America, and, in the beginning of the twentieth century.
   (b) Those immigrants who migrated in sixties and seventies after the immigration policies in these countries were modified.
   (c) Those who migrated to Thailand. This includes Punjabis and Gorakhpiris.

The cultural, contextual and situational conditions of these different categories of migrants differed significantly, and their bearing on the sandwich culture of these people has been examined in the following pages:

1. Indentured Labour in Trinidad

Indians from different regions such as United Provinces and Oudh (now Uttar Pradesh), Bihar, Central Provinces (now Madhya Pradesh) and a few from Bengal and South were recruited by the British, to work in their colonies as labourers. A large number of these people were poor and belonged to low caste, though there were few from higher castes such as Brahmans and Rajputs also. Majority of them were Hindus, though few Muslims and Christians were also there. Some of them were doing petty jobs but majority of them were poor agriculturists. Economically, all of them were not doing well as the Indian economy was affected badly by the Industrial Revolution in England. As the British banned the import of Indian goods to England which rendered a large number of Indian craftsmen unemployed. The conditions of the farmers also became precarious due to high land tax imposed by the British. Frequent famines in some parts of North and East India added to their miseries. The caste factor further deterred these people to accept other occupations besides the traditional occupations permitted by the caste. All these factors forced the Indians to accept the jobs offered by the British and their agents. The motivation for agreeing to do indentured labour was the hope that this may give economic relief to family members left behind. A large number of these immigrants were illiterate males and came from joint family. The mother tongue of these people was Hindi or Bhojpuri, though a few also spoke Tamil , Telugu and Bengali.

Under the indentured system Indians were bound to accept the terms and conditions of the employer, and were not permitted to leave or even change the employer. After the expiry of their contract, if they decided to stay, their legal status would remain same. Any one who infringed the rule was liable to be prosecuted as criminals and sentenced to prison. They were also not allowed to leave their places of work without a written permission from the employer. The physical conditions of their places of residence were also wretched. They were inhabited in small rooms of 10 feet by 10 feet in which two to four adults stayed. There was no privacy and cooking was done on the front steps. Even the medical facilities provided to them were precarious and the ration of rice or flour, ghee or split beans was not enough to fill their bellies. Till 1855, females were not allowed to join their husbands or other family members, and even when allowed only forty women for each hundred men were embarked. A few Indians took Negroes women as wives or mistress and competed against each other for the available women.

The condition under which Indians were brought to Trinidad and the condition they faced in Trinidad did not allow them to have much interaction with the Negroes as well as the White people. Language was the main barrier as an interpreter was required even at work. The British never directly interacted with Indians and it was only through middle man that they were communicating with them. Chances of opening apertures were almost non-existent but on the other hand insulatory mechanism were more in operation. Even when their contract as indentured labour was over, no apertures were created and situation did not change. Economically also they were at the lower rung of the scale. Neither Indians nor Whites and Negroes made any attempt to create apertures while in Trinidad. Certain cultural traits of the East Indians in Trinidad, did not allow them to develop personal contact with other ethnic groups. The process of revival of Indian culture began once they were free from indentured contract and the process enhanced after India became independent in 1947. This encouraged them to open their own schools, and also built mosques and temples and made arrangements to teach Hindi and Urdu to their children. Though only small percentage of Indians were able to understand the dialogues of Hindi movies, even then they preferred to watch them, because they found it closer to their lives and confirm to their basic values. Indian music was a regular features in wedding and other festivals. Thus, it can be inferred that they did not made any attempt to adapt the cultural traits of the host society and maintained their own identity. Despite the strong cultural ethnic cleavages and feeling of racial exclusiveness the tolerance level of Indians has been appreciated (Malik, 1971 and Braithwaite, 1954). In fact both have placed Trinidad society at Gordon's tolerance level of cultural pluralism. According to M.M. Gordon, "At the tolerance level of group relations ethnic groups would maintain such a high degree of social isolation from each other that virtually all primary contacts would be within the ethnic group and most secondary contacts would be either correspondingly confined or it across ethnic lines, completely accommodating, various ethnic groups would be encouraged to have a tolerant attitude towards one another" (Gordon, M.M., 1959: 829, quoted from Malik, 1971: 24).

Indians though belonged to different castes and ethnic groups revived number of their key institutions, which helped them to reproduce and maintain the basic elements of their native culture. This was considered a necessity if they wanted to maintain their distinct identity as "East Indians in their value orientation, life goals, beliefs and institutional structures differ from other ethnic groups with respect to marriage, family, kinship, way of life, religious ceremonies, festivals, dance and music they have distinctive traditions and customs" (Malik, 1971: 7). Brahmans who came as indentured labour, though their number was small, played pivotal role in revising Indian traditions and customs which were of immense help to maintain their identity as Indians. Even those well to do Indians in urban areas of Trinidad who had accepted some aspects of Western culture did not accept the Creole cultural values of Negroes.

In Trinidad, East Indians and Negroes tolerated each other without having any social interaction and also did not use violence against each other. Therefore, we can safely say that Indians remained Indian and maintained their distinct identity despite being in Trinidad for many years. They were at the minimum level of sandwich culture.

2(a). Early Immigrants to the United States of America

Indians who migrated to the United States of America in the beginning of the twentieth century were primarily poor peasants who mainly hailed from Jalandhar and Hoshiarpur districts of Punjab, besides a few soldiers who were in the British army during First World War. A major chunk of these people were followers of Sikh religion, but a small number of Hindus were also there. They migrated to these countries mainly due to high pressure of population on land and the fragmentation of land which led to uneconomic landholdings. By migrating to foreign lands these people wanted to help their family members back in India in order to improve their economic status. Migration of one member of family also encouraged and motivated the other members to migrate. The presence of some family members in a foreign land played significant role in the adjustment of new arrivals as they were provided all help including financial assistance.

The attitude of Americans, where the early Indian immigrants had settled, was not encouraging. They refused to regard Indians as a part of the American society as they spoke different language and wear turban and keep beard. Though the interaction between Americans and Indians was very limited, yet the Americans developed more and more negative attitude towards Indians with the increase in their number. The Americans considered Indians as people with low moral standards who shop lift and also cheat whenever they get chance. They also smell bad, as they do not take bath regularly and have lice in their hair. Their most common complain against Indians mainly Sikhs was that they did not even try to learn the language and that hampers their assimilation process in American society. The Americans also did not appreciate that their money was used to teach Punjabi language in schools. Americans did not like that the Indians have maintained their separate identity and always stick together helping each other. But this attitude was not shared by all Americans. Those who had some personal contacts with Indians liked them as individuals.

The negative attitude of Americans towards Indians did not dampen their spirit as they were economically better off as compared to what they were in India before migrating to America. They also encouraged their children to make use of the opportunities available to them in order to compete with others to achieve high status. The Indians appreciated the openness and fairness of American institutions and also enjoyed the rural atmosphere, rich farm land and good weather. They also admired the American education system which provided professional training to all including immigrants. The attitude of Indians towards Americans was mixed; as some of them had bad experience. But majority of them tried to play down the negative and prejudiced behaviour of some Americans, as it did not have much affect on their day-to-day activities.

The cultural background of these early immigrants to the United States of America did not allow them to have social interaction with the people of the host society. Being illiterate and poor, they lacked confidence and also did not speak the language to intermingle with the locals. The language barrier along with their dressing pattern including turban especially that of Sikhs forced these immigrants to insulate themselves from the local people and thus they preferred to live together in groups, which played significant role in maintaining their own cultural and religious identity. Even those who might have attempted to develop social relations with local people, the negative and prejudiced behaviour of these people played significant role to insulate immigrants from locals. The circumstances also encouraged the immigrants to built their own temples and Gurdwara which became a place of social gathering besides serving as an agent of cultural transmission to their children. Thus, these early immigrants did not create apertures which might have allowed them to adopt some aspects of the host culture.

As they were not able to create apertures, the insular mechanisms became strong. The derogatory remarks against these people in America forced these people to interact among themselves and also revived their Indian values. Though they encouraged their children to learn the language of the host society, yet at the same time taught them their mother tongue. Extra arrangements were also made in schools to teach Punjabi to these children, which was not appreciated by the local people. In Gurdwara all the programmes were conducted in Punjabi. First generation people could not develop any taste for the food of the host society, though they allowed their children to have food of the host society, if they liked so. But at home only Indian food was cooked. In terms of marriage also, they maintained their tradition and managed to get an Indian spouse for their wards. Despite opposition from local people, even teasing of children in school for wearing turban, the Punjabis did not discard their diacritical symbols such as turban, and also did not cut their hair short. They also maintained regular contacts with the people back in India.

In nutshell, it can be inferred that these early immigrants did not adapt non-material cultural aspects of the local people such as their ethics, values including food habits but accepted material culture such as automobiles and refrigerators, etc. as they found that these items are quite useful. On a ten-point scale of sandwich culture, they will also be at the bottom of the scale.

2(b). **Indian immigrants in USA in Sixties and seventies**

The conditions under which Indians in sixties and seventies migrated to USA and the conditions they encountered in the host society and their personal experiences differed vastly from the earlier immigrants. Majority of these new immigrants were educated professionals and experts in their own field of specialization and had command over English language. In fact, command of English language proved quite beneficial to these people for their settlement in an alien society. Some of these people, who were married, first came alone, but after sometime brought their families. Those who were not married, some of them went back to India to marry a person selected by their family members. This was true for both males as well as females. There were a few others who preferred to find an Indian spouse in these countries ignoring the caste and regional factors. There were few cases where Indian males married a White American girl. Some Indians went for inter-caste and inter-regional marriages such as a Kayastha boy from U.P. married a Maharashtrian Brahman girl from Mumbai. The early settlers had to struggle to settle in these countries as well as to maintain their religious and cultural identity. But by the time these new settlers came there were already large number of regional, religious as well as cultural organizations of Indians which acted as an agent of cultural transmission not only for the children of new settlers but were also handy for maintaining their own identity as Indians. In addition, there were a number of temples and Gurdwaras already established there which helped them to maintain their religious identity. These people also migrated with the intention of settling permanently in these countries.

The attitude of host people was not negative and hostile as was in the case of early settlers. These new immigrants were also keen to intermingle with the local people in these countries. Since these people were not discriminated, their attitude towards host people and culture was also positive which was quite crucial in their adjustment in a new environment.

The contextual and the situations conditions of these migrants provided them more opportunities to create apertures in these countries. These immigrants had the command over English language and therefore had no problem of communication. Some of them also shorten their long names in order to facilitate locals in pronouncing their names. These people also developed a taste for food of the host society, but at the same time did not alter their food habits entirely. At home most of these peopled cooked Indian style food but outside home, they have no problem in having the food of host society. So it was a mix of Indian and the cuisine of the host society. There are very few cases where Indians have married foreigners, and in majority of such marriages, the Indian males have married an American girl. Very few cases of Indian girl marrying foreigners were found. No case of religious conversion was found among Indians, though some Sikh males cut their hair short and became clean-shaven and also stopped wearing turban. But on their visits to India they will retain their original style of dress including turban.

These people have created more apertures as compared to the earlier settlers, but the insulatory mechanisms did not allow them to assimilate in the host society. These people have not only retained their mother tongue but also took steps to teach the language to their children, sometime by arranging special classes and also they took them to religious and other Indian functions where they interacted with other Indians. Since Indian food is served in all these functions children had no choice but to enjoy the food. Indians also preferred to settle close to each other and sometime circumstances forced them to settle close to each other.

Indians settled in USA were not very particular about the caste endogamy especially those who decided to marry an Indian girl already in the country. But those who went back to India to get married, invariably married a girl selected by the family members who belonged to the same caste. By and large, Indians maintained their caste endogamy except in few cases where inter-caste marriages took place.

Parents in most of the cases took special care to expose their children especially those who are born and brought up in the country to their own culture. Besides exposing them to their mother tongue and Indian cuisine they also took steps to make children aware of the religious and cultural aspects. They participated regularly in various functions organized by religious and cultural organization and also took children with them. On their visits to India they always purchased books and other reading material for their children. Despite all the measures, the second-generation people created more apertures as compared to their parents. They not only developed the taste for good of the host society but liked their music and films. In fact, some persons of second generation have described themselves as coconut, white from inside but brown from outside and this sums up the entire story.

2(c). **Indians in Thailand**

The emerging sandwich cultures of Punjabis (both Hindus and Sikhs) and Gorakhpuris differ significantly not only due to their places of origin in India, but also difference in their social and cultural ethos. Since the motives of migration of both these groups differed significantly their adaptation to Thai culture also varied accordingly. Since Punjabis both Hindus and Sikhs came for permanent settlement, their attitude and behaviour was altogether different from that of Gorakhpuris whose main aim was to earn and leave. In this section the adaptation pattern of Punjabis and Gorakhpuris have been summarized.

Since Gorakhpuris did not come for permanent settlement, though most of them are living there for many years, they did not even attempt to develop social relation with Thais except learning the language which was a necessity for their survival. Learning of language was necessary whether you are employed or are running your own business, in both the cases they have to interact with Thais. Some of the Gorakhpuris kept Thai women as concubines but did not marry them. To select a marriage partner for their children they always depended on their relatives back in India and most of the time they sent their teenaged daughters to India for education so that they are not exposed to Thai culture. They regularly maintained contact with relatives in India, and some people whose families were in India also remitted money. Most of the Gorakhpuris did not bring their family to Thailand and in some cases family visited for short duration especially during summer holidays when schools are closed in India. Quite a few Gorakhpuris used to wear their traditional dress of dhoti and kurta and did not change to pant and shirt. Gorakhpuris women continued to wear sari in traditional style where as young girls like salwar and kameez. They saw that their children learn Hindi besides learning Thai. They also watched Hindi movies on television and also enjoy Hindi films songs. On the whole it can be said that except language Gorakhpuri did not even attempt to socially interact with Thai people. Most of them cooked their own food as they did not like the smell of Thai cuisine, besides they were not sure whether it is pure vegetarian or what kind of cooking oil has been used. Their level of sandwich was limited to learning of language. Gorakhpuris followed their religion seriously and also contributed and participated in temple ceremonies.

Punjabis, both Hindus and Sikhs mainly migrated from West Punjab which became part of Pakistan after partition of India in 1947, came for permanent settlement and had open mind towards Thai people. Some of the Punjabis have taken Thai citizenship and according to Thai law changed their name. But on their visiting cards, both Indian as well Thai names are printed and generally they are identified by their Indian names. Those who have taken Thai Citizenship are residing in Thailand for three generations. The forefathers of these people migrated to Thailand. Most of them of the present generation are born and brought up in Thailand. Besides learning the language, most of them especially the younger generation have developed liking for Thai food, but at home Indian food is preferred. As far as marriages are concerned they also try to find a match within their caste and religion, but failing that they are ready to ignore caste factor. Their girls are not ready to marry Indian boys back in India as they are not ready to settle in India after marriage. Some well to do Punjabi families select match for their wards from other countries such as Singapore and Malaysia.

There are few cases among Punjabis, where they have accepted, Thai girl as their daughter-in-law but no case of Indian girl marrying a Thai boy was found. In terms of religion, both Hindus and Sikhs follow it strictly and also participate regularly in the functions of Gurdwara and temples. They also keep small space reserved in their homes for keeping the photos or statues of various gods and goddesses. In Sikh houses invariably one will find a picture of Golden temple in Amritsar and a picture of Guru Gobind Singh and/or Guru Nanak the founder of Sikh religion.

Punjabis also like to watch Hindi movies though some young children are found of English movies. All of them enjoy Hindi films songs. Since most of them migrated along with their all relatives, their visits to India are not frequent. They visited India on rare occasions.

Punjabis, both Hindus and Sikhs did not have much reservations about Thai people as compared to Gorakhpuris. Though both the groups are sandwiched between two cultures, yet they are at different level of sandwich culture.

Overview

In the preceeding pages we have discussed how the cultural, contextual and situational factors affected the adjustment and adaptation process of immigrants in an alien society. Whether the immigrants be assimilated in the host society or will remain sandwiched between the two cultures will depend on these conditions. However, it has been found that despite the variations in these conditions, the Indians are not anxious to assimilate but would prefer to retain their cultural and religious identity. In the process they are sandwiched between the host culture and the culture of the parent society, as they have to make adjustment and adopt a few traits of the host culture for survival. Now, in this sections, on the basis of data culled from various studies we have examined the hypotheses proposed in the first chapter.

Learning of the language of the host society is an important cultural trait which the immigrants have to learn for their survival. In the United States of America English is the main language of communication. Indians who migrated in sixties and seventies to USA, were educated professionals and had command over English language, and did not face any problem in communication with the people in the host society. As compared to these, Indians who migrated in the beginning of the twentieth century were illiterate who could not speak any language except Punjabi. These people took the help of some of their own men who had some familiarity with the English language. Those who went as indentured labour did not communicate directly with the employer but used the middleman. Gorakhpuris and Punjabis who migrated to Thailand, it became essential for them to learn the language in order to carry out their economic activities. Thus, the learning of language of the host society is a necessary condition for survival. All immigrants have to make some kind of adaptation. In case they are unable to develop the command over language, they have to learn at least some local terminology for survival. Learning of the language also does not affect the cultural and religious values of the immigrants and thus most of them do not object to learning of language. Learning of the language of the host society is a must, but Indian immigrants also take necessary steps not only to keep their mother tongue alive but also see that their children learn their mother tongue in addition to learning the language of the host society. To transmit the mother tongue, generally following measures are adopted:

1. Using the language at home while interacting among themselves including children. The presence of grand-parents further facilitate the process.
2. Some special arrangements are made either in school or in a temple or Gurdwara to teach the mother tongue.
3. Parents ask their children to accompany them to temples and Gurdwaras where all ceremonies are held in native language.
4. Children are also taken to cultural programmes and other functions and parties organized by Indians where children interact with other children.
5. Children are also exposed to native language through films, music and books.

In brief, it can be said that parents take all steps to expose their children to their mother tongue. As a consequence most of the children become bilingual. Even in terms of language they are sandwiched.

Though the adaptation of the cuisine of the host society is not essential for the survival of immigrants, yet a large number of Indians are not rigid in their attitude especially for the sake of children. Leaving aside a few Indians like Gorakhpuris in Thailand, majority of the Indians allow their children to eat the food of the host society if they so like. Though almost in all the Indians homes in all the countries and irrespective of their economic position Indian style cooking is preferred. However, in some homes it may be the mixture of Indian and the food of the host society.

One area where Indians irrespective of their religion, caste and region, are not ready to create apertures is the intermarriages between the host society and the migrants. Indians while selecting a mate for their wards give first preference to a person of the same caste and religion. They, by and large, discourage their wards to marry a person of the host society, but there are few cases where Indians males have married foreigners. But the cases of Indian females marrying foreigners are very few. One change which has been observed among Indians is that after living for many years in foreign country they are not very rigid about caste endogamy. This means that parents do not object if a Maharashtrian Brahman girl marries a Kayastha boy from Uttar Pradesh but may object her marriage to a foreigner. As the marriages between the Indian immigrants and the people of host society are not encouraged the chances of assimilation of Indians in the host society become remote. Since assimilation is not possible they will remain sandwiched between the two cultures.

All Indians, irrespective of their cultural conditions under which they migrated and the contextual and situational conditions they encountered in the host country, maintain regular contact with the people back at home, in one way or the other. Differences though exist in the nature and degree of contact. Early migrants to USA, remained in continuous contact with the family members left behind. They not only remitted money to their people in India, but also tried to get their other members. They also depended on their relations in India to get a suitable match for their wards. The educated professionals who migrated in sixties and seventies also maintained their contact with the family members in India. Even those who migrated along with their family members as Punjabis did in Thailand they kept their contact with India intact. Despite not having continuous contact with people in India, Indians in Trinidad maintained their traditions intact and revived them once they were free from contract.

Indians also visit India to attend family functions such as marriage or death in the family. A few Indians who have migrated along with their family members such as Punjabis in Thailand visit India for pilgrimage. By such visits, indirectly they expose their children who were born and brought up in foreign countries to Indian culture. In some cases family members visit India more frequently than the head of the family. Indians also invite their primary relatives especially their parents and siblings to visit them. All these visits make them nostalgic about Indian culture and acts as a insulator to the culture of the host society. This also reduces their chances of assimilations and thus they will remain sandwiched between the two cultures. However, Indians who migrated as indentured labour could not visit India or remain in touch with people back home.

The Indian immigrants who went either as indentured labour or migrated on their own to USA, or Thailand had to encounter many problems including discrimination for survival. In some cases Sikhs were the main target due to their distinct physical diacritical mark such as turban and long hair. They were ridiculed as well as tortured at least by a few people. The attitude of the people of host society was considered as a threat not only to their survival but also to their livelihood. In order to battle out the threat it became necessary for them to join hands and to form some kind of associations. Initially they used to meet informally to tackle the problem but gradually the associations were formed. As the number of immigrants swelled the number of associations also increased. Earlier there used to be only one association for all the Indians but gradually more and more associations were formed not only on the basis of religion, but also on the basis of caste, region and even language.

Slowly these associations expanded from social and cultural activities to religious activities. They also look the responsibilities to built temples and Gurdwaras which are used not only to revive their cultural and religious identity, but are also used to transmit their cultural and religious values and ethos to younger generation. These associations also came handy to later migrants to maintain their own identity. Some of these associations took responsibility to teach the languages. For instance, in Gurdwara arrangements are made to teach Punjabi. Moreover, all the activities in these places are held in Hindi, Punjabi and thus the younger generation are exposed to the language of the parent society. These associations and organizations played significant role not only in the revival but also in the continuation and perpetuation of the culture, religion and language of the parent culture.

The earlier migrants and those who migrated as indentured labour belonged to poor families. Even the Gorakhpuris in Thailand fall in this category. The main aim of all these people was to earn and then return to the parent society. Though all of them intended to return, yet actually very few of them returned. From the very beginning these people were conscious of their status and the contextual conditions further supported their apprehension of lower status. Such people adopted only those aspects of the host society such as language which was necessary for their survival. Besides they also started using the material cultural of the host society but kept away from non-material cultural and religious activities.

The adaptation level of the professionals and other educated people as well of those who established themselves as leading businessmen in the host society is higher as compared to the others. Firstly these people had more chances of interaction with the people of the host society and were also not averse to accepting some aspects of the host culture such as food, dress, etc. Secondly it was also necessary for them to accept those cultural aspects which were not hurting their basic values. The acceptance of the cultural aspects of these people was higher in comparison to others though these people are also sandwiched between the two cultures, but their level of rigidity and traditional values is less. At the same time they also earned some name and fame which also forced them to have positive attitude towards host culture.

People whose grandparents migrated to foreign countries and those who were born and brought up in the new environment and belong to fourth and fifth generation are trying to create more apertures. Since their socialization is done in different environment not only at home but also in the neighbourhood, their attitude towards host culture is totally different. In fact, majority of them considered the country of their birth as their own society and behave like that. Their schooling also exposed them to the cultural and other aspects of the host society. In fact, some of these people have not even visited India or there might be some people who might have visited once or twice in their lifetime. Such people are more prone to be a part of host culture. Some of these people compare themselves with coconut, i.e. brown from outside and white from inside. These people are really sandwiched between the two cultures and their level of sandwich will be sixty or seventy per cent.

People migrate in pursuit of better opportunities especially for economic gains. Indians also migrated to other countries in order to improve their economic status and to achieve that they were ready to accept any kind of jobs, sometimes on lower wages and ready to work for long hours. This was the bone of contention between the locals and the Indian immigrants in USA. The locals also did not like that the way the Indian immigrants were sharing boarding and lodging arrangements. The locals also held Indians responsible for depriving them of jobs by accepting lower wages. Since the Indians were regarded as the rivals of the locals and also due to their distinct social and cultural characteristics which were altogether different from the locals, Indians encountered discriminations in all these countries. Thus, the seeds were sown in the initial stages of the migration of Indians which deterred them to develop favourable attitude towards host culture. Thus, the question of their assimilation was a foregone conclusion.

In a country like Trinidad, where the number of Indians migrants was substantial, they also fought to achieve political power in addition to economic power. It is generally believed that economic power position may also be used to gain political power. In our study only in Trinidad Indians formed their political party in order to have power which they considered essential for their survival. The immigrants who may like to dominate economically and/or politically over the locals have to encounter criticism and negative attitude of the host society which will reduce their chances of assimilation.

Summing Up

Indian immigrants are not a homogenous group even if they belong to same State, religion, and caste and socio-economic strata. Despite all these, some common adaptation pattern of these people can be ascertained as a group at the place of their settlement. An attempt has been made to classify these people in the nine-fold classification given in the first chapter.

Indians who went as indentured labour neither had opportunity nor they were allowed to intermingle with the people of host society and therefore they can be put in the last category of our nine-fold classification given in the first chapter. Even their cultural conditions as well as contextual conditions did not permit them to open apertures. In fact, the conditions were ideal for insulation. Even after becoming free from indenture contract they continued with their earlier practices and avoided interaction with locals. On a ten-point scale of sandwich culture they will be at the lowest level.

In the second category we can put the early migrants to the United States. The cultural conditions of these people was no different than that of indentured labour except that these people choose their own destinations and also the time to travel. Since majority of these people were Sikhs their physical cultural diacritical factors insulated them from the host society. Being illiterate there was language barrier as they could not communicate with anybody except their own people. Besides, their customs and culture also played major role in insulating them from the host society. The host society people did not like that they have been invaded by strange people. Most of the host society people were hostile to Indians and which did not allow Indians to open apertures. Thus neither immigrants nor host society people made any attempt to create apertures. As a consequence Indians insulted themselves from the host society. These people can also be placed along with the Indentured labour.

Another group of Indians are those who migrated in sixties and seventies to USA. Majority of these people were keen to have open apertures and to some extent even the host society people were not averse to them. This group knew the language of the host society and did not have much problem in accepting their food. Economically, these people were better placed as compared to earlier migrants. In matters of marriage and religion they maintained their traditions and did not open apertures. Their transnational network also insulated them from opening apertures. But these people interacted with the locals and locals also were not hostile. Thus their level of sandwich culture will be higher than the earlier people. In a nine-point scale they can be placed at level five.

The younger generation of these people especially those who were born in those countries and were naturalized citizens of these countries wanted to have equal status as that of host society people. But were disillusioned when they were not accepted by the host society. This attitude frustrated most of them and they called themselves as Coconut brown from outside and white from inside. These were adopted most of the cultural traits of the host society but very few developed marital relations with them. In terms of religion also they did not go for conversion. These people can be placed at level three.

Punjabis and Gorakhpuris in Thailand were at different level of sandwich culture. Gorakhpuris can be placed at level nine where neither of the group is willing to integrate. Majority of the Gorakhpuris did not accept any traits of the Thai culture except language which was necessary for survival. But Punjabis, both Hindus and Sikhs are more open and even Thai people are also not hostile to them. In fact, Punjabis have played significant role in the development of Thailand. These can be place at the level five.

All these indicates that Indians irrespective of the conditions under which they migrated and the conditions they faced in the host society experiences are not ready to compromise on their identity. But in order to survive in an alien society they have to make few adjustments and adopt those cultural traits of the host society which are necessary and do not adversely affect their cultural and religious identity. The factor of "Basic Personality Structure" plays significant role in maintaining the immigrants their own cultural identity. According to Kardner, "certain culturally established techniques of child treatment had the effect of shaping basic attitude...and that these attitudes enjoyed a permanent existence in that mental equipment of the individual" (1945: III). The seeds of basic personality are sown in the early stages of the socialization process. The values learned in the family become a part of the basic personality structure of an individual and these values are nurtured and nourished by various ethnic, religious and linguistic network in a foreign country. Children born and brought up in these alien countries develop these values directly or vicariously and retain their identity, which prevent them from assimilating in the host society. As a consequence, the majority of Indian immigrants irrespective of their cultural, contextual and situational conditions are sandwiched between the parent culture and the culture of the host society. However, the nature and degree of sandwich will differ from group to group as well as from country to country.

Appendix

Trends of Indian Diasporic Studies

The spurt of studies of Indian diaspora in the last one and half decade is indicative of its emergence as an important field of investigation for social scientists though the curiosity to know the social and economic conditions of indentured labour from India who were hired to work in British colonies in the Carribean and the Asia Pacific region (which began in 1838), was there from the beginning. But interest in diaspora gained momentum since 1990s when large number of professionals from India who migrated to the Western countries in sixties and seventies faced the problems of identifications of their children born and brought up in those countries. The questions were raised whether these second generation of migrants are Indians or the nationals of the country of their birth. The cultural adaptation of these people dominated the studies on Indians abroad. However, the first note on emigration from India to Trinidad was prepared by D.W.D. Comins in 1893. The first study of Indian indenture labour in Fiji was in the form of an independent enquiry conducted by C.F. Andrews and W.W. Pearson in 1916. The problems of Indians in South Africa were highlighted by P. Subrahmanya Ayyar in 1925. The conditions of Indian labour in the neighbouring countries of Burma (now Myanmar) had been discussed by A. Rao (1933) and Bertie Reginald Pearn in 1946. Besides indentured labours that were hired as workers there were other Indians who migrated on their own. Some of these migrated to Western countries whereas there were others who migrated to British colonies for business. The problems faced by Indians in Western countries especially in Canada have been highlighted by Mehar

Chand in his book *Sikhism in Canada* in 1916. Most of the earlier studies concentrated on indentured labour but after 1960s the focus shifted to Indian migrants in United Kingdom, United States of America, and Canada.

In this section a content analysis of 715 references collected from various sources especially from Jain (1993) and Jayaram (2009) has been attempted to highlight the trends of studies on Indian diaspora. The content analysis has been attempted to look for the following:

1. Trends of diasporic studies of Indians settled in different countries and how it has changed over the years?
2. What aspects have been covered in these studies?
3. What is the overall trend of diasporic studies?

Out of 715 references included in the analysis more than 55 per cent, numbering 395, are in the form of articles in the books and journals and remaining 320 (45%) are books. Year-wise distribution of these publications is given in Table 1.

Table 1: Year-wise growth of Indian diasporic studies

Year	Articles	Books	Total	Average per year
Before 1960	12	10	22	–
1960-64	9	12	21	4.2
1965-69	19	14	33	6.6
1970-74	15	17	32	6.4
1975-79	25	11	36	7.2
1980-84	29	19	48	9.2
1985-89	47	40	87	17.4
1990-94	78	63	141	28.2
1995-99	59	60	119	23.5
2000-04	86	62	148	29.6
2005-06	14	9	23	4.6
Year not known	2	3	5	-
Total	395	320	715	15.0

Before 1960, scholars were mainly describing the conditions of indentured labour in different British colonies but the emphasis shifted from 1960s onwards from indentured labour to other Indian migrants in the Western countries of Canada,

United Kingdom and United States of America when the immigration policies in these countries were modified allowing more migrants from India, mainly the professionals. In fact, the year 1960 can be identified as the major turning point when social scientists began focusing more on migrants who selected their own destination and also the time of migration. The year-wise distribution of studies shows that its growth was gradual as in between 1960-64 only 21 studies averaging 4.2 studies per year appeared. The average before 1960 must be much less as only 22 studies were published. In the twenty-year period, between 1960 and 1980, a total of 122 studies with an average of 6.1 studies per annum were published but in the next ten years, between 1980 and 1990, the number almost doubled (13.5 studies per year). In the next fifteen years, i.e. from 1990 to 2004, the average jumped to 27.2 per year. The interest in Indian diaspora got impetus from 1990s when in five years more than 28 studies per year were published. The peak touched between 2000-04 when number of studies per year reached 29.6. Overall, 15 studies appeared every year between 1960 and 2006.

The analysis shows that there are more articles than books on the Indian Diaspora. In the beginning, there was not much difference in the number of articles and books except during 1960-64 (12 books and 9 articles) and 1970-74 (17 books and 15 articles) when number of books published was more than articles. Again during 1995-99, out of 119 publications 60 were books. Before 1980, the number of books published every year was less than four but between 1985 and 1989 the number increased to eight books per year; after that, in the next fifteen years more than 12 books were published every year. This further confirms that spurt in diasporic studies came after 1985.

Country-wise distribution of studies of Indian diaspora is given in Table 2.

Country-wise distribution of Indian diasporic studies reveals that about one-fifth of the total studies have been conducted on indentured labour in the Caribbeans and their Trinidad was the most researched country. The period between 1985 and 1999 was the most productive period of Caribbean studies as about 64 per cent of the studies were published during that period. Initially, the studies concentrated on the social and economic conditions of the Indian labour but after independence of Trinidad attention shifted to other aspects.

About fifteen per cent of the studies have been done on Indian migrants in Asian subcontinent. Malaysia and Ceylon (now Sri Lanka) were the countries where large number of people from Tamil Nadu were taken by the British to work in plantations. Among Asian countries large numbers of studies have been conducted on Indians in Malaysia. Other Asian countries where Indians have settled and researched are Myanmar, Indonesia, Nepal, Pakistan, Singapore and Thailand.

Another subcontinent where Indians migrated initially was Africa. The majority of studies have been conducted among Indians settled in South and East Africa followed by Uganda, Natal, and British Guyana. In all, about ten per cent of the studies have been done on Indians in Africa.

Fiji in Pacific was the other place where Indians were imported as indentured labour; in fact, the process of indentured labour started from Fiji. Indians in Fiji have also been studied by many scholars. Overall about 50 per cent of the total diasporic studies have been conducted on indentured labour settled in Africa, Asia, Caribbean and the Pacific.

Of the remaining, about 24 per cent of the studies have covered Indian migrants in Canada, United States of America, United Kingdom, Australia and New Zealand. Migration to Australia and New Zealand is relatively recent development. Data in Table 2 reveal that the studies of Indians in USA began from 1975 onwards, whereas in United Kingdom such initiative was taken as far back as 1960. The Indians in Canada also drew the attention of scholars from 1970 onwards. The first study of Indians in Australia appeared in the 1980s.

The countries of the Middle East attract workers from Asian subcontinent but do not grant them permanent status. Since 1985 scholars have started examining the impact of workers on the family and community once they returned back.

Table 2: Country and year wise coverage of diasporic studies countries

Year	African countries	Asian countries	Caribbeans	Canada	USA	UK	Pacific	Australia and New Zealand	Middle East	Others	Total
Before 1960	8	3	2	2	-	-	6	-	-	1	22
1960-64	6	4	5	-	-	2	2	-	-	2	21
1965-69	8	8	8	-	-	3	3	-	-	3	33
1970-74	8	8	6	5	-	3	2	-	-	-	32
1975-79	4	4	7	6	2	6	5	-	-	2	36
1980-84	1	11	7	14	8	-	4	1	-	2	48
1985-89	5	8	25	8	9	9	6	2	3	12	87
1990-94	16	27	35	4	7	7	4	2	7	32	141
1995-99	7	8	29	3	12	3	4	5	7	41	119
2000-04	10	20	13	13	11	10	7	5	5	54	148
2005-06	-	3	1	1	5	2	-	-	1	10	23
Year not known	-	-	2	-	-	-	2	-	-	1	5
Total	73	104	140	56	54	45	45	15	23	160	715

It may also be clarified that the State of Kerala has sent maximum workers to the countries of Middle East. This is one area which is drawing the attention of social scientists. There are large numbers of countries in Europe where Indians have settled and gradually their adaptation and adjustment have also been examined as about 22 per cent of the studies fall in this category. This also includes theoretically oriented studies.

Thematic Analysis

Depending on the titles of the publications ten themes have been identified. The themes are: (i) study of community and groups, (ii) studies covering social, cultural, economic and political aspects, (iii) religion based studies, (iv) study of indentured labour, (v) studies in historical perspective, (vi) theorizing diaspora, (vii) migration studies, (viii) identity question, (ix) race and ethnic related studies, and (x) miscellaneous studies. Year and theme-wise distribution is given in Table 3.

Table 3: Year and theme-wise* distribution of Studies

Theme

Year	1	2	3	4	5	6	7	8	9	10	Total
Before 1960	10	5	2	3	-	-	-	-	-	2	22
60-64	13	6	-	1	-	-	1	-	-	-	21
65-69	12	15	2	-	-	-	-	1	-	3	33
70-74	16	13	-	-	-	-	1	2	-	-	32
75-79	8	13	3	2	-	3	2	1	1	3	36
80-84	23	16	6	1	-	-	1	-	-	1	48
85-89	30	12	12	9	2	3	7	3	6	3	87
90-94	54	23	18	10	-	5	3	5	19	4	141
95-99	42	19	16	11	1	1	8	4	13	4	119
2000-04	64	30	16	3	2	4	-	10	19	-	148
05-06	10	6	-	-	-	-	1	1	3	2	23
Year not known	2	2	-	-	1	-	-	-	-	-	5
Total	284	160	75	40	6	16	24	27	61	22	715

* 1 community & groups, 2 social/cultural/economic/political, 3 religion, 4 indentured labour, 5 historical perspective, 6 theorizing diaspora, 7 migration, 8 identity question, 9 race/ethnic studies, 10 miscellaneous.

As specified earlier, themes have been worked out on the basis of the title of the publication. For instance, where only name of the community and group has been mentioned, all such studies have been included in the first category, whereas studies of specific aspects have been included in their respective categories. The thematic distribution shows that 63 per cent of the total studies cover first two categories. About 40 per cent of the total studies have been conducted on communities and groups without specifying any particular area. In other words, it is possible that scholars might have covered more than one aspect in these studies. Since it was not possible to go through each and every study they have been put in this category. More than 22 per cent of the studies have covered specific area—social, cultural, economic and/or political. About ten per cent of the studies researched on the religious aspects of the migrants, these are followed by 8.5 per cent studies on racial and ethnic relationship. Identity questions were raised in about four per cent of the studies. Around three per cent of the studies covered some aspect of migration. Studies in other areas are few.

Year-wise distribution of studies reveals that up to 1975 concentration was on two areas, i.e. community and groups and social, cultural economic aspects as more than 83 per cent of studies up to 1975 were done on these aspects. Before 1975, there were only four studies that discussed the religious aspects of migrants but gradually the number increased and out of total 75 studies on religion more than 82 per cent were done between 1985 and 2004. Same was the case with racial and ethnic studies. More than one-third of the studies on identity were conducted between 2000-04. This shows that focus of studies on Indian diaspora varied according to the developments in the countries of settlement.

Analysis shows that studies of communities and groups have drawn the maximum attention. In USA, 63 per cent of the total studies have been done on communities and groups, followed by 58 per cent in UK, 49 per cent in Asian countries, 46 per cent in Canada, and 45 per cent in African countries. The maximum studies of social, cultural, economic, and political aspects have been conducted among indentured labour in the Caribbeans especially in Trinidad followed by Asian countries where 36 per cent of the total studies relate to this area. 45 per cent of the total studies in the Caribbean are on religious aspects compared to 35 per cent in Asian countries. In the Pacific countries 30 per cent of the total studies were on communities and groups and 22 per cent studies are on racial and ethnic aspects. In the Caribbean, only 11 per cent of the studies were on racial and ethnic aspects.

Country-wise distribution of thematic studies shows that maximum coverage of communities and groups was given to Indian migrants in Asian countries as 18 per cent of the total studies fall in this category (Table 4). Indians in USA with 12 per cent comes next followed by Africa (11.6%), Caribbeans (10.2%), and nine per cent each in Canada and UK. Among social, cultural, economical and political studies caribbeans with one fourth of the studies in this area dominated followed by 15 per cent studies of migrants in Asian countries. In African countries ten per cent of the studies covered this aspect. In rest of the countries it was less than ten per cent. Other area which occupied dominance place among Indian migrants was the changes in the religious aspects. Being a traditional and caste bound society Indians were very particular to maintain their religion despite the problems faced especially by indentured labour. Initially they were unable to maintain their religious practices but once they were free from indentured contract they revived their religious practices. The migrants to Western countries did not face any such problem.

Distribution of studies on religious aspects reveals that 45 per cent of the total studies in this were conducted among Indians in Caribbean countries specially in Trinidad. Next in line was the religious aspect of migrants in Asian countries. There were clashes between Indian migrants and the locals in Trinidad and Fiji. 43 per cent of the studies on race and ethnic relations have been done in these two countries. There were clashes in Malaysia and Sri Lanka among Asian countries and in Africa as well as in UK; some scholars have also examined racial and ethnic aspects in these countries.

Table 4: Theme and country-wise distribution of studies countries

Themes	Africa	Asia	Caribbeans	UK	Pacific	USA	Canada	Australia and New Zealand	Midde East	Others	Total
Communities & groups	33	51	29	26	15	34	26	15	6	49	294
Social/Cultural Economic/Political	16	24	39	7	7	9	8	-	5	45	160
Religion based	5	12	24	6	5	6	6	-	-	11	75
Indentured Labour	9	5	13	-	5	-	-	-	-	8	40
Historical	-	-	1	-	-	-	4	-	-	1	6
Theorizing	-	-	-	-	-	-	-	-	-	-	16
Migration	-	-	8	-	3	5	4	-	4	-	24
Identity	2	5	5	-	-	-	3	-	-	12	27
Race/ethnic Relations	6	7	16	4	10	-	-	-	-	18	61
Others	2	-	5	2	-	-	5	-	8	-	22
Total	73	104	140	45	45	54	56	15	23	160	715

Following groups and communities have been studied. Since nothing was specifically mentioned in the title all have been put in one category. The distribution of groups and communities is: Indians (118), Asians (46), Sikhs and Punjabis (29), women (19), Hindus (18), Muslims, Christians and other Minorities (21), Tamils (10), Professionals (8), Coolie (6), and Others (9). Since Indians who were taken as indentured labour did not belong to any particular community and group, majority of the studies of Indians have been conducted in these countries.

Under social, cultural, economic and political aspects the area covered are Cultural (34), Political (32), Economic (30), Family, kinship and marriage (21), Caste (17), Social change (6), Food habits (4), and others (16). Maximum studies under religion were on Hindu and Hindisuim (33), followed by religion and culture (13), temples, gods and goddesses (10). There were few studies on Sikhism, Christianity, and Islam. Studies on indentured labour covered the experiences and the conditions under they were living, and also the violence which took place at the place of residence, and few studies on indentured women.

The analysis of trend studies of Indian diaspora shows that the most of the scholars have concentrated either on indentured labour in Carribeans especially in Trinidad and/or on the migrants in the Western countries of Britain, Canada and the United States of America. There are very few studies of Indian diaspora in other countries. There is an urgent need to conduct studies on Indian diaspora in other countries including Australia and New Zealand.

Endnotes

1. Published in *Sociological Bulletin* in 1989.
2. For details see Atal, Yogesh and Luca Dall'Oglio, *Migration of Talent: Causes and Consequences of Brain Drain,* Unesco Regional Office, Bangkok, 1987.
3. *Ibid.*
4. Indenture refers to under a restrictive contract of employment for a fixed period in a foreign country in exchange for payment of passage, accommodation, and food. The term "indenture" itself came to be used because the skin on which contracts were traditionally written in duplicate were divided with an indented edge, so that each side would fit into the other.
5. There is a famous Hindi novel on this system focusing on Indians in Mauritius. Authored by Giri Raj Kishore, it is titled *Pahla Girmitiya.*
6. Stevedora Spanish word for persons employed at loading and unloading ships; for longshoremen. For Coolies.
7. Now spelt as Awadh.
8. Manas, *The Indian Diaspora, At home in Trinidad*, 2009 taken from Internet.
9. A few years back a team of Indians musicians from Trinidad gave performance in Delhi in which steel drum and chutney music were used. They sung Hindi film songs without knowing the meaning of most of the words they used. I attended this function.
10. It is called Kakkars, five items all named with the initial letter "Ka" are prescribed for Sikh males. A Sikh is supposed to wear Kanga (comb), Kesh (hair—no haircut and shave), Katar (dagger), Kara (bracelet), and Kachchh (underwear). These are his dress diacriticals.
11. At that time Thailand was a part of Southeast Asia. Thai's original home was somewhere in China. Due to continuous pressure from Chinese they migrated towards the West and Northwest of Yunnan. The first Thai state was founded in 650 A.D. called Nan Chao which flourished till 13th century when it was overpowered by Mongols. The first Thai

dynasty kingdom was founded in 1239 AD called SukhoThai to the North of Chiangmai. It was the place where Thais met the Khmers, the Burmese, and the Mons who were already exposed to Indian culture. It is through these people that Thais were exposed to Indian culture. In 1350 a new Thai state was founded towards the south of SukhoThai. First it was located at Suphan Buri and later on shifted to Ayudha which was destroyed in 1767 by the Burmese army. General Taskin, the leader of Thai army reorganized his followers and freed Ayudha from Burmese occupation in 1776. Instead of Ayudha he selected Thonburi, a city south of Ayudha as the new capital. After the execution of General Taskin in 1782 General Chao Phraya Chakri became king and shifted his capital to Bangkok. Since then Bangkok is the capital of Thailand and Chakri dynasty are the rulers.

References

Abella, Manolo I. and Yogesh Atal (eds) (1986). *Middle East Interlude: Asian Workers Abroad*, Bangkok, UNESCO Regional Office.

Agarwal, Priya (1991). *Passage from India; Post 1965 Indian Immigrants and Their Children: Conflicts, Concerns and Solutions*, Palos Verdes, Yuvati Publications.

Andrews, C.F. and Pearson, W.W. (1916). *Indentured Labour in Fiji: an Independent Enquiry*, Calcutta, Star Printing Works.

Angelo, Michael (1997). *The Sikh Diaspora: Tradition and Change in an Immigrant Community*, New York, Garland Publishing Inc.

Anwar, Muhammad (1998). *Between Cultures: Continuity and Change in the Lives of Young Asians*, London, Routledge.

Ashfaq, Ali Syed (1984). *Indians Overseas*, Bhopal, Jai Bharat Publishing House.

Atal, Yogesh and Luca Dall'Oglio (1987). *Migration of Talent: Causes and Consequences of Brain Drain*, Bangkok, UNESCO Regional Office.

Atal, Yogesh (1989). "Outsiders versus Insiders: The Phenomenon of Sandwich Culture" in *Sociological Bulletin*, Vol. 38, No. 1.

Atal, Yogesh (2001). "Managing Multiciplcity: The Insider-Outsider Duality" in *Economic and Political Weekly*, Vol. XXXVI, No. 36.

Aurora, G.S. (1968). *The New Frontier Man: A Sociological Study of Indian Immigrants in the United Kingdom*, Bombay, Popular Prakashan.

Aurora, G.S. (1991). *Indian Emigration*, New Delhi, Puja Publisher.

Bacon, Jean (1996). *Lifelines: Community, Family and Assimilation among Asian Indian Immigrants*, New York, Oxford University Press.

Bahadoorsingh, Krishna (1968). *Trinidad Electoral Politics: The Persistence of the Race Factor*, London. Institute of Race Relations.

Bahadur Singh, I.J. (1979). *Other India,* New Delhi, Arnold-Heinemann Publishers.

Bahadur Singh, I.J. (ed) (1987). *Indians in the Caribbean*, New Delhi, Sterling Publishers.

Barrier, G.N. and Dusenbery, V.A. (1989). *The Sikh Diaspora: Migration and the Experience Beyond Punjab*, Columbia, South Asia Books.

Bhardwaj, Surinder, M. and N. Madhusudana Rao (1990). "Asian Indians in the United States: A Geographical Appraisal" in Colin Clarke, Ceri Peach and Steven Verovec (eds) *South Asians Overseas Migration and Ethnicity*, Cambridge, Cambridge University Press.

Bonacich, Edna (1973). "A Theory of Middleman Minorities" in *American Sociological Review*, Vol. 38, pp. 583-94.

Braithwaite, Lloyd (1954). "The Problem of Cultural Integration in Trinidad" in *Socio and Economic Studies*, Vol. 3, No. 1.

Braithwaite, Lloyd (1960). "Social Stratification and Cultural Pluralism" in *Annuals of the New York Academy of Sciences*, Vol. 83.

Brereton, Bridget (1974). "The Experience of Indentureship 1845-1917" in La Guerre, John G. (eds.) *Calcutta to Caroni: The East Indians of Trinidad Bristol*, Longman.

Brown, Richard Harvey and George V. Caelho (eds) (1987), *Migration and Modernisation: The Indian Diaspora in Comparative Perspective*, Williamsburg.

Cady, John F. (1966). *Thailand, Burma, Lacos and Cambodia*, New Jersey, Prentice Hall INC.

Cady, John F. (1964). *South-East Asia: Its Historical Development*, New York, McGraw Hill.

Chand, Mehar (1916). *Sikhism in Canada*, Vancover, Vancover University.

Clarke, Colin (1986). *East Indians in a West Indian Town: San Fernando, Trinidad 1930-1970*, Boston and Sydney: Allen and Unwin.

Clarke, Colin (1967). "Caste among Hindus in a Town in Trinidad: San Fernando" in Barton M. Schwartz (ed) *Caste in Overseas Indian Communities*, California, Chandler Publishing Company.

Clarke, Colin, Ceri Peach and Steven Vertovec (1990). "Introduction: Themes in the Study of the South Asian diaspora" in Colin Clarke, Ceri Peach and Steven Vertovec (eds.) *South Asian Overseas Migration and Ethnicity*, Cambridge, Cambridge University Press.

Coedes, G. (1966). *The Making of South-East Asia*, London, Routledge and Kegan Paul (Translated by H.M. Wright).

Coedes, G. (1968). *The Indianized States of South-East Asia*, Honolulu, East-West Centre Press (English edition).

Coelho, George V. (1958). *Changing Images of America: A Study of Indian Student Perception*, Illinois, The Free Press.

Comins, D.W.D. (1893). *Note on Emigration from India to Trinidad*, Calcutta, Bengal Secretariat Press.

Cole, W. Owen and Piara Singh Sambhi (1978). *The Sikhs: Their Religious Beliefs and Practices*, New Delhi, Vikas Publishing House.

Coughlin, Richard J. (1960). *Double Identity: The Chinese in Modern Thailand*, Hong Kong, Hong Kong University Press.

Coward, Harold et al. (ed) (2000). *South Asian Religious Diaspora in Britain, Canada and the United States*, Albany, State University of New York Press.

Crocombe, Ron (ed.) (1981). *Pacific Indians: Profiles from 20 Countries*, Suva, Institute of Pacific Studies, University of South Pacific.

Cumpston, I.M. (1953). *Indian Overseas in British Territories, 1883-1854*, London, Dawson of Pall Mall.

Dabydeen, David and Samaroo, Brinsley (ed) (1987). *India in the Caribbean*, London, Hansib Publishing.

Daniels, Roger (1994). "The Indian Diaspora in the United States" in Judith M. Brown and Rosemary, Foot (eds) *Migration: The Asian Experience*, Oxford, St Martin Press in association with St. Anthony College.

Desai, Prakash N. and George V. Coelho (1980). "Indian Immigrants in America: Some Cultural Aspects of Psychological Adaptation" in Parmatama Saran and Edwin Eames (eds). *New Ethnics, Asian Indian in the United States*, New York, Praeger Publishers.

Desai, Santosh N. (1980). *Hinduism in Thai Life*, Bombay, Popular Prakashan.

Dookeran, Winston (1974). "East Indians and the Economy of Trinidad and Tobago" in La Guerre John (ed) *Calcutta to Caroni: The East Indians of Trinidad*, Bristol, Longman.

Dwarka Nath (1950). *History of Indians in British Guiana*, London, Thomas Nelson.

Eisenstadt, S.N. (1954). *The Absorption of Immigrants*, London, Routledge and Kegan Paul Ltd.

Fisher, Maxine P. (1980). *Indians of New York City: A Study of Immigrants from India*, New Delhi, Heritage Publishers.

Furnival, J.S. (1948). *Colonial Policy and Practice: A Comparative Study of Burma and Netherlands*, Delhi, Cambridge.

Gandhi, Rajnikant S. (1974). *Locals and Cosmopolitans of Little India: A Soiological Study of the Indian Student Community at Minnesota*, Mumbai, Popular Prakashan.

Gibson, Margaret A. (1988). *Accomodation Without Assimilation Sikh Immigrants in an American High School*, Ithaca, Cornell University Press.

Girling, John L.S. (1981). *Thailand: Society and Politics*, Ithaca, Cornell University Press.

Gordon, M.M. (1959). "Social Structure and Goals in Group Relations" in M. Berger (ed) *Freedom and Control in Modern Society*, New York, D. Van Nostrand and Co.

Gordon, M.M. (1964). *Assimilation in American Life: The Role of Race, Religion and National Origin*, New York, Oxford University Press.

Gosine, Mahin (1993). "East Indians in Trinidad and their Inter-ethnic Relations" in Jagat K. Motwani, Mahin Gosine, Jyoti Barrot-Motwani (eds) *Global Indian Diaspora: Yesterday, Today and Tomorrow*, New York, Global Organization of People of Indian Origin.

Gregory, Robert G. (1993). *South Asians in East Africa: An Economic and Social History, 1890-1980*, Boulder, West View Press.

Gupta, Anirudha (ed) (1971). *Indians Abroad, Asia and Africa*, New Delhi, Orient Longman.

Gupta, Surendra K. (1999). *Indians in Thailand*, New Delhi, Books India International.

Haraksingh, Kusha R. (1988). "Structure, Process and Indian Culture in Trinidad" in Howard Johnson (ed) *After the Crossing: Immigrants and Minorities in Caribbean Creole Society*, London, Frank Cass.

Helweg, Arthur W. and Helweg, Usha M. (1990). *Immigrant Success Story: East Indians in America*, Delhi, Oxford University Press.

Hussain, Zakir (1982). *The Silent Minorities: Indians in Thailand*, Bangkok, Bangkok Social Research Institute, Chulalongkran University.

Jain, Ravindra K. (1970). *South Indians on the Plantations Frontier in Malaya*, New Haven, Yale University Press.

Jain, Ravindra K. (1986). "The East Indian Culture in a Caribbean Context: Crisis and Creativity" in *India International Centre Quarterly*, Vol. 13, No. 2.

Jain, Ravindra (1989). "Race, Relations, Ethnicity, Class and Culture: A Comparison of Indian in Trinidad and Malaysia". *Sociological Bulletin*, 38 (1).

Jain, Ravindra K. (1993). *Indian Communities Abroad: Themes and Literature*, New Delhi, Manohar.

Jain, Ravindra K. (1993). "Bibliography" in Ravindra K. Jain *Indian Communities Abroad: Themes and Literature*, New Delhi, Manohar.

Jain, Ravindra (1998). "Indian Diaspora, Globalization and Multiculturalism: A Cultural Analysis". *Contributions to Sociology*, 32 (2).

Jayaram, N. (2000). "The Dynamics of Language in Indian Diaspora: The Case of Bhojpuri/Hindi in Trinidad" in *Sociological Bulletin*, Vol. 49, No. 1.

Jayaram, N. (2003). "The Politics of 'Cultural renaissance' among Indo Trinidadians" in Bhikhu Parekh, Gurharpal Singh and Steven Verovec (eds). *Culture and Economy in the Indian Diaspora*, London, Routledge.

Jayaram, N. (2006). "The Metamorphosis of Caste among Trinidad Hindus" in *Contributions to Indian Sociology*, Vol. 40, No. 2.

Jayaram, N. (2009). "The Study of Indian Diaspora (1989-2006)" in Yogesh Atal (ed). *Sociology and Social Anthropology in India*, New Delhi, Pearsons.

Jayaram, N. (2009). "References" in N. Jayaram, "The Study of Indian Diaspora (1989-2006) in Yogesh Atal (ed). *Sociology and Social Anthropology in India,* New Delhi, Pearsons.

Jha, J.C. (1974). "The Indian Heritage in Trinidad" in La Gherre John (eds) *Calautta to Caroni: The East Indians of Trinidad*, Bristo, Longman.

Johnson, Howarded (1988). *After the Crossing: Immigrants and Minorities in Caribbean Creole Society*, London, Frank Cass.

Judge, Paramjit S. (1993). *Punjabis in Canada: A Study of Formation of Ethnic Community*, Delhi, Chanakya Publication.

Kannabiran, K. (1998). "Mapping Migration, Gender, Culture and Politics in the Indian Diaspora: Commemorating Indian Arrival in Trinidad", *Economic and Political Weekly*, 33 (44).

Kardiner, A. (1945). "The Concept of Basic Personality Structure as an Operation Tool in Social Science" in Ralph Linton (ed). *Science of Man in the World Crisis,* New York, Columbia University Press.

Khandelwal, Madulika (2002). *"Becoming American Being Indian: An Immigrant Community in New York*, Ithaca, Cornell University Press.

Klass, Morton (1961). *East Indians in Trinidad: A Study of Cultural Persistence*, New York, Columbia University Press.

Klass, Morton (1991). *Singing with Sai Baba: The Politics of Revitalization in Trinidad*, USA West View Press.

Kondapi, C. (1951). *Indian Overseas*, 1838-1949, New Delhi, Indian Council of World Affairs.

Kumar, R. Gopa (2003). "Indian Diaspora and Giving Patterns of Indian Americans in USA" in R. Gopa Kumar (ed). *Indian Diaspora and Giving Patterns of Indian Americans in USA*, Kumar, New Delhi, Charities Aid Foundation India.

Kurian, George and Ram P. Srivastava (1983). *Overseas Indians: A Study in Adaptation*, New Delhi, Vikas Publishing House.

LaBrack, Brucps (1983). "The Reconstitution of Sikh Society in Rural California" in George Kurian and Ram P. Srivastava (eds). *Overseas Indians: A Study in Adaptation*, New Delhi, Vikas.

La Guerre, John Gaffar (2003). "Convergence and Divergence in the Organization and Politics of Two Plural Societies: Guyana and Trinidad and Tabago" in Sarva Daman Singh and Mahavir Singh (eds), *Indians Abroad*, Gurgaon, Hope India Publication.

La Guerre, John Gaffar (ed) (1974). *Calcutta to Caroni: The East Indians of Trinidad*, Trinidad, Longman Caribbean.

Leaf, Murray J. (1972). *Information and Behaviour in a Sikh Village: Social Organization Reconsidered*, Berkeley, University of California Press.

Leonard Spark, P. Saran and Karen Gusberg (1980). "Indian Immigrant in America: A Demographic Profile" in Parmatma Saran and Eames Edwin (eds), *The New Ethnics: Asian Indians in the United States*, New York, Praeger Publication.

Leonard, Spark and Isaksen Karen (1992). *Making Ethnic Choices: California's Punjabi, Mexican Americans*, Philadelphia, Temple University Press.

Linda, Mary (2001). 'Constructing Identity': Hindu Temple Production in the United States in T.S. Rukmani (ed). *Hindu Diaspora: Global Perspectives*, New Delhi Munshiram Manoharlal.

Maharaj, Ashram B. (1991). *The Pandits in Trinidad: A Study of Hindu Institutions*, Couva, Trinidad, Indian Review Press.

Maira, Sunaina Marr (2002). *Desis in the House: Indian American Youth Culture in New York City*, Philadelphia, Temple University Press.

Majumdar, R.C. (1963). *Hindu Colonies in Far East*, Calcutta, Firma K.L. Mukhopadhyay (Second edition).

Malik, Yogendra K. (1971). *East Indians in Trinidad: A Study in Minority Politics*, London, Institute of Race Relations.

Manas (2009). *Indians Diaspora, At home in Trinibad* (Taken from internet).

Mani, A. (1993). "Indians in Thailand" in K.S. Sandhu and A. Mani (eds) *Indian Communities in South East Asia*, Sujapore, Institute of South Asian Studies.

Mann, Gurinder Singh (2000). "Sikhism in the United States of America" in Harlod Coward (ed) *The South Asian Religion*

Diaspora in Britain, Canada and the United States, New York, State University of New York Press.

Merton, Robert K. (1972). "Insiders and Outsiders: A Chapter in the Sociology of Knowledge" in *The American Journal of Sociology*, Vol. 78, No. 1.

Mishra, Ruchira (2004). "India in Thailand" in Surendra K. Gupta (ed), *Emerging Social Science Concerns*, Delhi, Concept Publishing Company.

Mohammed, Patricia (2002). *Gender Negotiations Among Indians in Trinidad 1917-1947*, Houndmills, Palgrave.

Motwani, Jagat K. (ed) (1993). *Global Indian Diaspora: Yesterday, Today and Tomorrow*, New York, Global Organization of People of Indian origin.

Nandan, Yash and Edwin Eames (1980). "Typology and Analysis of the Asian Indian Family" in Parmatma Saran and Edwin Eames (eds), *The New Ethnics: Asian Indians in the United States*, New York, Praeger Publications.

Nevadomsky, Joseph (1983). "Changes Over Time and Space in the East Indian Family in Rural Trinidad" in George Kurien and Ram P. Srivastava (eds), *Overseas Indians: A Study in Adaptation*, New Delhi, Vikas.

Niehoff, Arthur (1967). "The Function of Caste among the Indians of the Oropuche Lagoon, Trinidad" in Barton, M. Schwartz (ed) *Caste in Overseas Indian Communities*, California, Chandler Publishing Company.

Nikongo, Ba'Nikongo (1994). "Of Afro-Trinidadians, Indo-Trinidadians and 'apartheid' in a pseudo-emancipatory, accidential Bi-racial State" in *The Eastern Anthropologist*, Vol. 47, No. 3.

Paranjape, Makarand (ed) (2001). *In Diaspora: Theories, Histories, Texts*, New Delhi, Indialog Publications.

Pearm, Berlie Reginold (1946). *The Indian in Burma Ledbury, England*, Le Play House Press, Race Relations Studies, No. 4.

Persaud, Paul (1979). "Indians in the Caribbean" in I.J. Bahadur Singh ed *The Other Indian*, New Delhi, Arnold-Heinemann.

Rangaswamy, Padma (2000). *Namaste America: Indian Immigrants in an American Metropolis*, Pennsylvania, The Pennsylvania State University Press.

Rao, A. (1933). *Indian Labour in Burma*, Madras, Keshari Printing Press.

Samaroo, Brinsley (1974). "Politics and Afro-Indian Relations in Trinidad" in John La Guerre (ed), *Calcutta to Caroni: The East Indians of Trinidad*, Longman.

Sandhu, K.S. (1973). *Early Malaysia*, Singapore, University Education Press.

Sangha, Sujinder Singh (2001). *Racial Equality, Education and Punjabis in Britain, England*, Punjabi Guardian Press.

Saran, P. and Philip J. Leonard Spark (1980). "Attitudinal and Behavioural Profile" in Parmatma Saran and Edwin Eames (eds) *The New Ethnics: Asian Indians in the United States*, New York, Praeger Publications.

Saran, P., B.N. Varma and Ainslie T. Embree (1980). "Hinduism in a New Society" in Parmatma Saran and Edwin Eames (eds), *The New Ethnics: Asian Indians in the United States*, New York, Praeger Publications.

Saran, Parmatma (1985). *The Asian Indian Experiences in the United States*, New Delhi, Vikas Publishing House.

Saran, Parmatma and Eames, Edwin (1980). *The New Ethnics: Asian Indian in the United States*, New York, Praeger Publishers.

Schwartz, Barton M. (1967). "The Failure of Caste in Trinidad" in Barton M. Schwartz (ed), *Caste in Overseas Indians Community*, California, Chandler Publishing Company.

Segal, Uma A. (2002). *Framework for Immigration: Asians in the United States*, New York, Columbia University Press.

Sharma, S.L. (1989). "Perspectives on Indians Abroad" in *Sociological Bulletin*, Vol. 38, No. 1.

Shastri, Satyavarat (1982). *Studies in Sanskrit and Indian Culture in Thailand*, Delhi, Perimal Publications.

Sheth, Pravin (2001). *Indians in America: One Stream, Two Waves, Three Generations*, Jaipur, Rawat Publications.

Singh, Kelvin (1974). "East Indians and the Larger Society" in La Guerre, John (ed) *Calcutta to Caroni: The East Indians of Trinidad,* Bristol, Longman.

Siu, Paul C.P. (1952). "The Sojourner" in *The American Journal of Sociology*, Vol. 58.

Smith, M.G. (1960). "Social and Cultural Pluralism" in *Annals of the New York Academy of Sciences*, Vol. 83.

Sonakul, Ayumongol (1982), "Unravelling the Case of the Indian Nut Vendor" in *The Bangkok Post*, March 26.

Srivastava, Ram P. (1983). "The Evolution of Adaptive Strategies: East Indians in Canada" in George Kurian and Ram P. Srivastava, (eds), *Overseas Indians: A Study in Adaptation*, New Delhi, Vikas.

Turner, J.H. and Edna Bonacich (1980). "Towards a Composite Theory of Middleman Minorities" in *Ethnicity*, Vol. 7, No. 2.

Vertovec, Steven (1990). "Oil Boom and Recession in Trinidad Indian Villages" in *South Asian Overseas Migration and Ethnicity,* Colin Clarke, Ceri Peach and Steven Vertoec, Cambridge, Cambridge University Press.

Vertovec, Steven (1994). "'Official' and 'popular' Hinduism in Diaspora: Historical and Contemporary Trends in Surinam, Trinidad and Guyana" in *Contributions to Indian Sociology*, Vol. 28, No. 1.

Vertovec, Steven (2000). *Hindu Diaspora: Comparative Patterns*, London, Routledge.

Warshaw, Steven (1975). *South-East Asia Emerges*, Berkeley, The Diably Press.

Williams, Raymond Brady (1988). *Religions of Immigrants from India and Pakistan: New Threads in the American Tapestry*, Cambridge, Cambridge University Press.

Williams, Raymond Brady (1996). *Christian Pluralism in the United States: The Indian Immigrant Experience*, Cambridge, Cambridge University Press.